Grease or Grit?

Grease or Grit?

International Case Studies of Occupational Licensing and Its Effects on Efficiency and Quality

Morris M. Kleiner
Maria Koumenta
Editors

2022

W.E. Upjohn Institute for Employment Research
Kalamazoo, Michigan

Library of Congress Cataloging-in-Publication Data

Names: Kleiner, Morris M., editor. | W.E. Upjohn Institute for Employment Research.
Title: Grease or grit? : international case studies of occupational licensing and its
    effects on efficiency and quality / Morris M. Kleiner, Maria Koumenta, editor.
Description: Kalamazoo, Michigan : W.E. Upjohn Institute for Employment
    Research, 2022. | Includes bibliographical references and index. |
    Summary: "The book provides a comprehensive approach to whether a dominant
    governmental institution in the labor market-occupational licensing-greases,
    which enhances, or on the other hand results in grit, which diminishes the efficient
    workings of labor and service markets in parts of Europe and the United States.
    The detailed case studies in the book indicate that an increase in the availability of
    service providers or enhanced competition does not have negative effects on the
    quality of the services provided, prices, or survey measures of consumer
    satisfaction" — Provided by publisher.
Identifiers: LCCN 2022026785 (print) | LCCN 2022026786 (ebook) | ISBN
    9780880996860 (paperback) | ISBN 9780880996877 (ebook)
Subjects: LCSH: Occupations—Licenses—United States. |
    Occupations—Licenses—Europe. | Labor market—United States. | Labor
    market—Europe.
Classification: LCC HD3630.U6 G74 2022 (print) | LCC HD3630.U6 (ebook) |
    DDC 331.120973—dc23/eng/20220728
LC record available at https://lccn.loc.gov/2022026785
LC ebook record available at https://lccn.loc.gov/2022026786

The facts presented in this study and the observations and viewpoints expressed are
the sole responsibility of the author. They do not necessarily represent positions of
the W.E. Upjohn Institute for Employment Research.

Cover design by Carol A.S. Derks.
Index prepared by Diane Worden.
Printed in the United States of America.
Printed on recycled paper.

For my beloved children and grandchildren, who always keep me curious about life's adventures.

– Morris M. Kleiner

For my beloved son Noah, whose infectious energy and smile made this book possible.

– Maria Koumenta

Contents

Acknowledgments

The authors in this book provide a nontechnical approach for practitioners, academics, and students of regulation who are interested in the role of institutions in labor markets. Taken together, the detailed case studies in the book indicate that an increase in the availability of service providers or enhanced competition does not have negative effects on the quality of the services provided, prices, or survey measures of consumer satisfaction.

We both want to especially thank the European Commission for helping fund the research efforts for many of the chapters in the volume. We also want to thank the staff of the Upjohn Institute for Employment Research, especially Kevin Hollenbeck and Brad Hershbein for comments on earlier drafts. We greatly appreciate the work by Allison Hewitt Colosky for her outstanding editing and comments that improved the content for all the authors in the volume. Richard Wyrwa offered insightful suggestions throughout the publishing process.

We both want to thank the authors in this volume for their efforts in developing the unique and creative research approaches that are developed in the book. Morris Kleiner wishes to thank colleagues at the Federal Reserve Bank of Minneapolis, the Humphrey School of Public Affairs, and the Center for Human Resources and Labor Studies at the Carlson School of Management, both at the University of Minnesota, and the National Bureau of Economic Research who provided many helpful comments. He also wants to thank Sally Mosow Kleiner for her encouragement and editorial support.

Maria Koumenta would like to thank colleagues at Queen Mary University, the London School of Economics, and the European Commission, as well as attendees at the 70th meeting of the Labor and Employment Relations Association for their helpful comments.

1
Introduction and Overview

Morris M. Kleiner
University of Minnesota

Grease in the gears of intricate machinery can make it operate more effectively, but grit in the gears will slow it down, and could dramatically reduce its efficiency. Analogously, government intervention in the operation of labor markets may make them operate more effectively—like grease—or may slow its workings—like grit (Groshen and Schweitzer 1999). In this book we examine for the first time in a comprehensive manner a dominant governmental institution in the labor market—occupational licensing—to evaluate the extent to which these regulations enhance or diminish the efficient workings of labor and service markets in the United States and parts of Europe (Kleiner 2006; Koumenta and Pagliero 2019). Occupational licensing is often referred to as "the right to practice." Under licensing laws, working for pay in a licensed occupation is illegal without first meeting government standards. Certification, another form of government regulation, provides a "right to title," which does not forbid others from providing the service but it prohibits the use of a specific title for working in the occupation.

This book examines occupational regulation from an international perspective across five countries and multiple services and occupations (Kleiner 2013). Our aim to provide both breadth and depth to the issues of the potential costs and benefits of service quality and efficiency in regulated service occupations.

The licensing of occupations is usually based on the protection of the public interest and service quality to society. It is rare, however, that such criteria are subjected to theoretical or empirical scrutiny. Existing literature on occupational regulation (Farronato et al. 2020; Kleiner et al. 2016) has documented the difficulty in developing measures of service quality. The ability to evaluate the influence of occupational licensing on quality outcomes has been difficult to assess for at least three reasons. First, quality is challenging to define and measure. For example, it is common to use consumer satisfaction to assess quality in the market, but solely relying on consumer satisfaction might provide insufficient information on the licensing-quality relationship. Second, the criteria of what constitutes good quality service varies greatly. Measures of quality usually depend on the occupation in question, thereby limiting the degree to which researchers can generalize from occupation-specific studies to the universe of occupations that are regulated. Consequently, it makes sense to focus on specific occupations. Third, limited data availability places significant constraints on what research questions we can address empirically, thereby compromising the scope for evidence-based evaluations. For example, prices, health, and education outcomes are often difficult measures to obtain from existing governmental and industry sources in Europe and the United States.

Some of the challenges to evaluating occupational licensing outcomes are related to methodology. There may be nonrandom and unobservable factors that confound attempts to identify the causal effect of occupational regulation on quality in empirical work. Studies from the United States often exploit between-state variations in licensing regimes, which enables researchers to undertake comparisons of the same occupation while controlling for other explanations of the observed effects. In the case of the European nations, these cross-national variations are more difficult to obtain.

In this book we evaluate and clarify the relationship between licensing and quality by using expanded definitions of quality. For example, the authors develop methods associated with effectiveness, consistency, nonexcludability, and affordability in service delivery. They operationalize these approaches by using a variety of measures associated with (a) the processes involved in service provision, (b) the outcomes of the services provided, and (c) other value-added proxies. They draw on regulatory changes and outcomes within occupations in Europe and the United States to empirically assess the effect of regulation on quality and illustrate different policy evaluation approaches.

Overall, this book seeks to answer the following empirical question: What is the relationship between occupational regulation and service quality? We use empirical case studies within and across nations and occupations to compare homogeneous groupings of workers and consumers within similar institutional frameworks. We take three unique

approaches in this volume to understand the national and data innova-
tions. First, we provide a variety of methods because there is more than
one way to address this question. Taken together, our case studies make
use of extensive empirical methods and data sources, all showing the
complexities associated with defining the measures of quality. Second,
owing to the unique nature of each occupation in the labor market and
the high heterogeneity in how quality can be defined and measured,
our approaches are good illustrative examples of how such important
research questions can be tackled. We do not offer a one-size-fits-all
solution to addressing these important policy dilemmas. Instead, our
goal is to draw attention to the challenges associated with undertaking
research of this kind, while at the same time empirically illustrate ways
in which these challenges and policy proposals can be addressed. Third,
we avoid thinking of occupational regulation as a binary state, which
not only captures observationally more common policy initiatives but
also imposes unnecessary and possibly socially suboptimal restrictions
on policy alternatives, such as the relaxation or tightening of regulatory
provisions. Including diverse forms of regulatory initiatives across con-
tinents will shed new light on the types of reforms that could be evaluated and implemented under different institutional frameworks.

COSTS AND BENEFITS OF REGULATION

Occupational licensing policies are a major source of labor market
regulation in the United States and Europe, which has potential costs—
licensing may reduce the supply of labor in licensed occupations and
drive up prices—and benefits—better product quality because of higher
levels of job-specific education and training. Despite the often-heated
debate over the trade-offs posed by licensing, economists and policy
analysts have offered little guidance on how to conduct a cost-benefit
analysis of such policies within different nations and across occupations.

The underlying rationale for the influence of occupational licensing
is that it affects both labor supply and demand for the services. Licensing influences supply by increasing the costs of entry and thus reducing
the number of persons in the occupation. Hours worked, however, may
increase as wages rise. The supply of workers in the case of occupa-

tional licensing can only increase by the number of individuals who go through the process to receive their license. The assumption is that government is influenced by the occupational organizations representing the workers in the trade, ranging from doctors to interior designers.

In contrast to the supply issues above, occupational licensing increases the demand for labor, since consumers perceive that the regulated services are of higher quality because of the increased job-specific training. The total supply of services to consumers is a function of the offsetting effects of falling labor supply and rising demand for the regulated service. Also determinative is whether consumers are willing to pay more for them. This volume attempts to address these issues.

PREVIEW OF THE STUDIES

The six case studies presented in this book delve into different areas of the influence of occupational licensing and measures of quality. The first four chapters break new ground by examining occupations practiced in European nations. Similarly, the last two chapters evaluate the influence of licensing on quality in health care and in beauty services for the United States. Below we preview the chapters and discuss how they contribute to the overall theme of whether regulations provide grease or grit in the quality consumers receive from particular services.

The first case study, by Morris M. Kleiner, examines how variations in the regulatory requirements imposed on the ridesharing firm Uber affect measures of quality outcomes for two cities, London and Dublin. Kleiner uses pricing, customer satisfaction, and safety, as measured by hard accelerations and hard braking. Kleiner's research finds little evidence that greater regulatory constraints (at least of the type observed in these two jurisdictions) improve ridesharing experiences or reduce prices for passengers. Further, the technological context within which the taxi and ridesharing driving professions operate is considerably different than was the case when the regulatory provisions for taxi drivers were initially instituted. Based on the evidence for this firm, a reassessment of the form that regulating entry to the taxi and ridesharing driving professions is undertaken may be in order. Further, occupations that have innovative technology can reduce information asymmetries, as is the case for London and Dublin. Consequently, reducing regulations may be an appropriate path for policymakers to take in considering regulatory labor policies in the face of new technologies.

Chapter 3, by Maria Koumenta and Mark Williams, examines a unique issue of entry into the profession of driving instructors in the United Kingdom (U.K.). Driving instructors are subject to compulsory training requirements, which in practice has led to a dual market where fully trained (licensed) and trainee (in the process of completing their training and obtaining a license) driving instructors could both legally offer instruction for payment. The government changed the requirements by trainee license holders since so few went on to become full instructors. As a result, they could no longer provide driving lessons for money unless they were accompanied by a fully licensed driving instructor, marking a shift from certification to de facto licensing.

Koumenta and Williams do not observe any increases in the pass rates of student drivers, leading them to conclude that the quality of driving instructors has not improved. Similarly, they do not find any improvement in three quality measures of consumer performance. For example, overall pass rates are negative once time trends are considered. These findings are reinforced when they compare the trends in pass rates for student drivers to those of motorcyclists before and after the reform proposals. Finally, they note an increase in the cost of driving lessons. The authors conclude that the introduction of licensing for U.K. driving instructors has not resulted in any improvement in service quality, and they discuss the implications for regulation policy.

In Chapter 4, Eva Pagano, Mario Pagliero, Emanuele Pivetta, and Lorenzo Richiardi examine the regulation of pharmacies in Italy and population health outcomes. In Italy, the work of pharmacists, the number and location of pharmacies, and the production, trade, and distribution of drugs are all heavily regulated. For example, the number of pharmacies and their locations are determined through administrative procedures. The authors use hospital admission record data at the municipality level, exploiting the change in the demographic rule that links the number of pharmacies to the number of inhabitants in the municipality. Pagano et al. find a significant effect of the availability of pharmacies on selected health outcomes, but the results show a negative impact of availability of pharmacies on the number of hospital admissions related to influenza.

Chapter 5, by Piotr Białowolski and Michał Masior, examines the deregulation of the legal professions in Poland. In 2004 and 2005, a set of activities reserved exclusively for those in the legal profession were relaxed, and in 2005 and 2009, entry restrictions and experience requirements, as well as passing scores for bar exam for lawyers, were reduced. Owing to the easing of entry into the legal profession, the number of advocates and legal advisors doubled between 2005 and 2015. Białowolski and Masior evaluate these changes through the lens of service quality. They also examine the number of reported complaints and disciplinary cases. The authors' analysis of complaints by the type of reported misconduct indicates that the frequency of the most common allegation, a breach of professional duties, fell by two-thirds following the reforms and opening of the profession to newcomers, while the frequencies of other types of reported breaches, including unethical behavior, remained stable or slightly declined. Overall, the relaxation of licensing for legal services greatly benefited the consumers of legal services.

The last two case studies focus on evaluations of the quality aspects of the influence of licensing for specific occupations in the United States. Kihwan Bae and Edward Timmons in Chapter 6 study the effects of expanding scope of practice for health service professionals on the quality of care received by patients. They review the existing literature and focus on advanced practice registered nurses—nurse practitioners and other nurse subspecialties. Although the literature has some limitations, there is an emerging consensus: allowing medical practitioners the ability to work independently from physicians does not reduce the quality of care. Bae and Timmons examine geographic and occupational correlations of scope of practice on health outcomes. If anything, the increase in independent practice appears to improve the quality of care with no measurable influence on prices. Despite these results, regulatory reforms on the scope of practice are often crippled by professional associations and their members who may benefit from existing regulations. They conclude by stating that the COVID-19 pandemic has provided both researchers and policymakers with an opportunity to further consider and investigate the implications of these health policy questions.

In Chapter 7, Darwyyn Deyo examines the effect of licensing on quality for two occupations related to beauty services: makeup artists and shampooers. These occupations are not licensed in every state, and the policy variation allows the author to study the effect of having stringent licensing requirements, such as the amount of licensing fees or board licensing exams, and the influence of having a license. The analysis examines businesses in licensed occupations (makeup artists and shampooers) with the ratings for an unlicensed occupation (pet groomers). Deyo finds that licensing requirements and the associated intensity do not significantly increase quality through the ratings measure of consumer satisfaction. She also finds evidence that licensing sometimes has a negative effect on quality—this result is clearer when businesses are separated by the number of reviews each one received. Licensing does not seem to measurably increase quality across the board or for all businesses, even within the same occupation. Under another set of estimates, licensing barriers reduce quality while also imposing entry barriers for workers and higher costs for consumers. The net effect is that licensing does not seem to reliably increase quality, as measured by consumer ratings. Deyo suggests that policy reform that reduces licensing barriers does not have to come at the cost of lower quality for consumers.

DIRECTION FOR THE VOLUME

Although each case study in this book examines the effect of licensing on efficiency and service quality, there is also a focus on labor market issues. First, occupational licensing has been found to raise wages only for licensed workers, reduce occupational and geographic mobility, and lower employment. Second, are there sufficient efficiency and service quality gains through these regulations to consumers to compensate society for these inefficiencies and barriers in the labor market (Kleiner 2015)? The goal of this book is to give the public, consumers, and students of the economy and labor market a detailed, nontechnical look at occupational licensing in Europe and the United States. The book examines the institution of occupational licensing from an international perspective, offers a view from the perceptions of consumers, and outlines some unintended consequences of policies that have arisen because of occupational licensing. The reader of this book should become a more informed member of a regulated occupation, consumer, student of regulation, or voter who can better determine the direction of policy that will help to evaluate whether occupational licensing serves as grease or grit in the operation of labor markets and service economies.

References

Farronato, Chiara, Andrey Fradkin, Bradley Larsen, and Erik Brynjolfsson. 2020. "Consumer Protection in an Online World: An Analysis of Occupational Licensing." NBER Working Paper No. 26601. Cambridge, MA: National Bureau of Economic Research.

Groshen, Erica, and Mark Schweitzer. 1999. "Identifying Inflation's Grease and Sand Effects in the Labor Market." In *The Costs and Benefits of Price Stability*, Martin Feldstein, ed. Chicago: University of Chicago Press, pp. 273–314.

Kleiner, Morris M. 2006. *Licensing Occupations: Ensuring Quality or Restricting Competition?* Kalamazoo, MI: W.E. Upjohn Institute for Employment Research.

———. 2013. *Stages of Occupational Regulation: Analysis of Case Studies.* Kalamazoo, MI: W.E. Upjohn Institute for Employment Research.

———. 2015. *Guild-Ridden Labor Markets: The Curious Case of Occupational Licensing.* Kalamazoo, MI: W.E. Upjohn Institute for Employment Research.

Kleiner, Morris M., Allison Marier, Kyoung Won Park, and Coady Wing 2016. "Relaxing Occupational Licensing Requirements: Analyzing Wages and Prices for a Medical Service." *Journal of Law and Economics* 59(2): 261–291.

Koumenta, Maria, and Mario Pagliero. 2019. "Occupational Regulation in the European Union: Coverage and Wage Effects." *British Journal of Industrial Relations* 57(4): 818–849.

2
Occupational Licensing Outcomes in the Face of Technological Change

Ridesharing in London and Dublin

Morris M. Kleiner
University of Minnesota

Two rapidly growing trends in the labor market are the expansion of occupational regulations imposed by the government and the growth of the on-demand or contingent workforce (Katz and Krueger 2016; Kleiner and Krueger 2010, 2013). The taxi industry and its drivers historically have been heavily regulated by governments in most developed countries. These regulations typically involve granting exclusive rights to provide cab services to firms and setting standards for its drivers. Usually, the services include quality controls (such as vehicle age and appearance), the imposition of entry restrictions for drivers (such as topographical knowledge tests), and the control of fares (Beesley 1973). The justification for these licenses has been public safety and consumer protections. From an occupational licensing perspective, the most common barrier to entry for individuals looking for work in the sector is the requirement that drivers be licensed by local governments. Ideally, a study seeking to address these questions would examine indicators of service quality before and after the removal of entry requirements to the occupation. However, since such deregulatory shocks are rare, an alternative approach is to focus on the differences in entry requirements for prospective drivers across jurisdictions. The recent increase in the number of ridesharing services, which compete with traditional taxi services, offers an opportunity to examine how differences in regulation affect quality outcomes.

Ridesharing services refer to rides provided by drivers for remuneration by passengers who order and pay for this service via a smartphone app, and these contractors are among the fastest growing markets of on-demand workers (Katz and Krueger 2019). Drivers use their own private vehicles, set their own hours, and in most jurisdictions have been considered private contractors who link onto the app.

This chapter uses data from Uber Technologies to examine how differences in regulations to become a ridesharing driver affect quality outcomes in London and Dublin. A key question is whether more relaxed regulation requirements to become a driver are associated with inferior services or quality. As the restrictiveness of the regulatory regime increases, does quality improve enough to justify this potentially costly regulatory intervention? How does the variation in regulations on ridesharing affect consumer satisfaction and measures of ride safety? The analysis shows how fares vary with the intensity of licensing requirements and compares the quality of rides in London, where entry to the occupation is more relaxed relative to heavily regulated "fully licensed" taxi drivers, and Dublin, where ridesharing drivers are subject to the same stringent requirements as those of "fully licensed" taxi drivers (Kleiner 2006).[1] The results of ridesharing in London and Dublin are measures of consumer satisfaction of a ride on a scale of one through five. Measures of vehicle hard starts and hard stops are measured in both percent and the number of hard starts per ride. Finally, prices are in dollars per standardized ride in both cities. Specifically, I use data from Uber Technologies to measure the influence of more relaxed regulations on consumer satisfaction with the service, measures of safety of the vehicle, and prices of rides. These outcomes should provide new evidence on how regulation affects service for ridesharing when there are major technological changes within an occupation.

OVERVIEW OF THE RIDESHARING INDUSTRY

Ridesharing became popular in 2010, as the use of smartphones became widespread, but there is limited research on the outcomes of these services. Most countries regulate the taxi industry by setting entry restrictions for drivers, operators, pick-up procedures, and vehicles (Schaller 2007). The theoretical rationale for taxi regulation is developed from the experience good problem: goods for which quality cannot be determined by the consumer until after the good has been consumed, giving rise to "moral hazard" (e.g., the provider overcharging, operating a substandard car, or taking a longer route, all because there are few consequences of providing lower-quality services). Regulation in the form of minimum standards setting is assumed to solve this imperfect information problem (Shleifer 2010). Proponents argue that regulation is vital to ensure customers do not experience longer trips and higher fares by using unscrupulous providers or have their safety compromised by dangerous driving or criminal behavior. Further, while they accept that price and supply controls might result in higher fares, this enables dense markets to cross-subsidize low-density ones while peak traffic cross-subsidizes off-peak service availability (Dempsey 1996). Without regulation, service to low-density and off-peak trips may decline or be unavailable. Critics of this approach argue that unregulated market entry and fares for taxi providers will shift the supply curve upward, resulting in lower fares, shorter waiting times, improved availability (especially in underserved markets), and greater entrepreneurial opportunities (especially for minorities and immigrants) (Cevero 1985).

From an empirical perspective, research has looked at the effect of regulatory changes on service availability and prices as they apply to the taxi service market in general and from a producer perspective. The removal of quantity controls on taxis in many U.S. cities, for example, caused supply to increase by an average of 19–23 percent (Dempsey 1996; Schaller 2007; Teal and Berglund 1987). Dempsey (1996) finds that in cities that abolished quantity and fare restrictions, prices in both cruising and dispatch markets rose by an average of 29 percent per year, but despite a slight initial surge in supply, service availability fell to pre-deregulation levels. More recent work by Rojeck and Masior (2016) analyzes the deregulation of entry to the taxi driver occupation in Poland that took effect in 2013. The reform included giving authorities the right to control pricing practices, as well as dropping the requirement of a preparatory course and exam in cities with populations over 100,000. This provided an ideal context for which to compare the effects of the reform between cities, but also before and after reform comparisons of the regulations relative to prices. The study finds that in those cities where barriers to entry were relaxed, prices after the reform fell for the first time, while the supply of taxis rose as measured by the number of licenses issued. Using quality indicators such as license withdrawals, complaints filed against taxi drivers, and frequency of malpractice, the authors find mixed results on quality.

In contrast to these previous studies, this chapter analyzes the regulation of drivers. In practice, entry to the occupations in different jurisdictions is covered by a wide spectrum of regulatory policies, and it is this variation in restrictiveness that is the focus of the chapter, specifically the levels of regulation rather than the existence of licensing.

Background on the Company and Cities Examined

Uber Technologies is headquartered in San Francisco, with operations in 633 cities worldwide. Its platforms can be accessed via its websites and mobile apps. Uber began its rides in San Francisco in 2010 and in New York City the following year. The technology company's business model was to match people needing rides with people who were willing to provide those rides for a price. Uber expanded outside the United States in 2013, and London became one of its largest and most successful operations, with about 40,000 drivers and more than 3.5 million customers. At different times the firm has had up to 80 percent of the total ridesharing market in London, the U.K., and the United States; the Dublin estimates have been harder to obtain (DMR Statistics 2017; *Financial Times* 2017). However, those numbers on market share have declined recently as more competitive substitutes have entered the ridesharing market.

The creation of an app and accompanying software facilitated the company's matching process and allowed valuable data to be collected that can compare indicators of quality for different levels of stringency in entry requirements for taxi drivers. The drivers pay a fee—a percentage of the ride—to Uber for using the matching process (Hall et al. 2019). Under this business model, ridesharing drivers pay a portion of their fares to the ridesharing platform operator (in this case Uber), a commission-based compensation model used by many internet-mediated service providers. To Uber drivers, this commission is known as the Uber fee. By contrast, traditional taxi drivers in most cities make a fixed payment independent of their earnings, usually a weekly or daily medallion lease, but keep the fare dollar net of expenses.

London and Dublin have both similarities and differences in how taxi and ridesharing services operate. For some historical background,

London's taxi service market has traditionally been served by two types of providers, namely the "black cab/hackney" drivers and "minicab" drivers. Black cab drivers have traditionally had a legal monopoly through taxi regulations to be the only service that can be called on the street through hailing a taxi or from a cab phone. In contrast, minicabs must be prebooked and are not allowed to be fitted with a taxi meter. The prebooking takes place via taxi service companies.

Prior to the COVID-19 pandemic, Uber was one of the most popular ways to book rides in London. At that point the city accounted for about 5 percent of Uber's global active user base of 65 million, and nearly a third of its active user base of 11 million in Europe. There were about 40,000 licensed Uber drivers in London who serviced about 3.5 million users. There is fierce opposition to Uber from the Licensed Taxi Drivers' Association, a union representing London's black cab drivers, whose drivers take several years to train for their job, in part by memorizing London's streets, a practice called the Knowledge. In contrast, the governmental entry requirements that exist for Uber drivers in London are the same as those that apply to the minicab drivers. These lower requirements have made entry into the ridesharing business as a supplier of these services much easier than traditional black cabs. Uber drivers use technology through the app in the car to find locations in London. The relatively high cost of training for drivers using the fully licensed black cab model has helped make Uber popular among prospective drivers in London. A four-mile trip in the middle of the week costs at least $24.00 in a black cab compared to about $11.00 with Uber (*Wall Street Journal* 2017). Uber was under threat of losing its license to operate in London but held on despite opposition by black cab operators (Satariano 2018). In 2021, Uber contractors came under U.K. labor laws with substantially greater wages and hours benefits (Satariano 2021).

Similarly, Dublin is also a capital city and is the largest city in Ireland. It is, however, much smaller than London, with a population of almost 2 million. The taxi sector in Ireland has traditionally been highly regulated, involving firm restrictions on the number of new vehicle licenses (i.e., licenses linked to the vehicle, not the driver) issued by the state (Barrett 2003). As the industry regulator, the National Transport Authority also has the power to control the number of licensed taxi drivers by setting the pass rate, exam fees, and other licensing requirements. Ireland's rapid economic growth in the 1990s and a booming tourist market increased demand for taxi services, but because of caps on the number of vehicle licenses that the state regulators were issuing, it resulted in increased customer discontent with the sector and its regulators (Barrett 2010). In 2000, the Irish High Court increased the size of the taxi sector by gradually raising the cap on vehicle licenses.

Uber's method of operation is different in Dublin. Irish law requires that anyone carrying passengers for pay must have a full taxi license. Consequently, Irish regulatory policy requires Uber drivers in Dublin to meet the same requirements as a fully licensed taxi driver. As a result, Uber drivers in Dublin are typically traditional taxi drivers who have also signed up to the Uber platform to work to attract additional customers either during or after work hours. One potential barrier to entry is that drivers must be licensed by local authorities, as is the case in both cities, and that the precise requirements vary across jurisdictions.

DRIVER LICENSING IN DUBLIN AND LONDON

The entry test for taxi drivers in Dublin is designed to verify that new drivers are familiar with good practice and have a solid working knowledge of the county in which they plan to operate.[2] The detailed and in-depth test consists of 90 questions in two sections:

1) The Industry Knowledge Module consists of 54 questions relating to industry regulations, vehicle knowledge, map reading, fares and charges, and customer service (including disability awareness and equality and diversity, business acumen and health and safety), as set out in the module's manual.

2) The Area Knowledge Module consists of 36 questions related to the administrative county in which one expects to be licensed. This aspect of the taxi licensing process is focused on examining driver familiarity with the area so that passengers' trips are provided in an efficient and safe manner.

Overall, the process of getting a license in Dublin is significantly more expensive compared to London because of the in-depth knowledge requirements. In addition to the tests, the driver also must produce a tax clearance certificate and undergo a criminal record and a medical check. The cost of the licensing process is approximately $448 and includes $109 toward the standard driver entry test, $303 toward the commercial driver license fee, and $36 toward the criminal records check fee.[3] The licenses need to be renewed every five years. These requirements typically apply to all taxi drivers in the city, including those that offer ridesharing services through the Uber platform.

The number of available vehicle licenses in Dublin is restricted, which has resulted in a decline in the number of active taxi driver licenses (from more than 47,000 in 2009 to less than 27,000 in 2016). The greatest number of restrictions occurred before 2013, and the number of licensed vehicles remained roughly constant after 2013. In London, the number of licensed taxi vehicles remained roughly constant during this time.[4]

The regulations for Uber drivers in London are the same as the driver of a "private hire" vehicle.[5] Specifically, the driver must be at least 21 years old, hold a full U.K. or European Member State driver's permit for at least three years, and, as of 2016, pass an English language test.[6] In addition, Uber drivers in London are required to undergo a criminal record check and a medical examination, as well as take a topographical knowledge test. The London exam differs substantially from the one in Dublin. It consists of five modules that assess the ability of prospective candidates to read maps and plan routes, as well as their general understanding of London's topography.

Table 2.1 compares the requirements to enter the market in London and Dublin. There is considerable variation between the two cities in terms of the barriers Uber ridesharing drivers face. These differences let us examine how variations in the stringency of regulation impact selected indicators of quality. Uber drivers are subject to licensing in both jurisdictions, since at least some requirements to enter the occupation are in operation, and these are legally binding. Consequently, Uber ridesharing drivers in London and Dublin are subject to what is referred to as occupational licensing in the academic literature on regulation (see, for example, Kleiner 2006, 2015; Koumenta and Pagliero 2016).

Table 2.1 Summary and Overview of Licensing Requirements for Uber Drivers in Dublin and London

	Dublin	London
Educational requirements	Area knowledge test Industry knowledge test Driving permit	Topographical knowledge test (based on map reading) Driving permit
Other entry requirements	Private hire license (issued by the National Transport Authority) Criminal records check Medical check Tax clearance certificate Minimum age of 18 years	Private hire license (issued by Transport for London) Criminal records check Medical check Minimum driving experience of at least three years English language test (where applicable) Minimum age of 21 years
Cost of driver licensing (approx.)	$448	$1,014
Renewal	Every five years	Every three years

DATA USED FOR THE ANALYSIS

Uber Technologies supplied the proprietary data, which can be used for research purposes. Unlike survey data, which may be collected with less care—an inaccurate response leaves virtually no economic consequences to the firm—this information is unique in that it is what the company uses for decision making and is collected and compiled with greater care. In all the analyses, trip-level data were used from November 2013 (Uber expanded to London in July 2012) through December 2016. The data were provided as part of the company's regular compilation of administrative information without any knowledge about how the data might be used for analysis or public policy purposes. Unfortunately, no data on tips are available, and since many times tips are given in cash, this may undervalue the cost of the ride to consumers. To provide a balanced sample for the two cities, the analysis uses the universe of 162,386 rides from Dublin. For London, Uber provided a random sample of 260,081, or 0.5 percent of all rides.[7] Appendix A contains the definitions of the variables in the data set.[8]

To evaluate the influence of regulation, I collected information from Uber on the following indicators. First, I obtained data on the quality of ridesharing through driver-quality ratings for the most widely used Uber service, UberX. After completing a trip, riders rate the driver on a scale of one star (lowest quality) to five stars (highest quality). The value is treated as a "measure of process" or satisfaction since it reflects the customer experience from the ride. Second, consumer safety is an important dimension of service quality. Uber made available two measures of safety: hard accelerations and hard braking on individual trips. Both have been shown to be some of the most predictive factors for car crashes and accidents (*Claims Journal* 2015). The values are obtained when drivers, who use the Uber app, have a passenger in the vehicle and have the app turned on. Uber drivers in London could usually take longer for the same distance or generally go on longer trips than in Dublin. Including a city dummy variable allows a measurement of the differences of quality of service that is not associated with differences in transit time or distance. For example, the quality of a ride could deteriorate because of heavy traffic but not because of differences in regulatory intensity. To account for these issues, the analysis controls include 37 dummy variables for year and month (as one variable); 6 dummies indicating day of the week (Sunday–Saturday); and 23 dummy variables for hour of travel. If heavy traffic occurs regularly at a given time during a day, these time fixed effects would pick this up. In addition to the time fixed effects, we control for location-specific effects. For instance, if a statistically identical driver in Dublin on a trip of identical duration and distance brakes more frequently using a busy road than in London on a four-lane highway, the behavior results from the characteristics of the road chosen for the specific trip, not from differences in regulatory intensity. To account for this, the analysis uses a set of 1,023 dummy variables clustering pickup and drop-off location by longitude and latitude (see Horton 2016).[9]

APPROACHES USED IN THE ANALYSIS

Table 2.2 shows the means and observations for the key variables for the two cities, Dublin and London. The means for trip duration and trip distance are similar, so one can make meaningful comparisons between them. Also, the observations are similar for both cities. As shown in the table, it is interesting, however, to find that London has a shorter estimated time of arrival at the client's pickup location, despite being a busier city with more traffic.[10] A likely reason for this is

Table 2.2 Means and Number of Observations for the Key Variables in the Analysis for Dublin and London

Variable	City	N	Mean
Trip duration (in seconds)	London	471,877	1,219.9190
	Dublin	456,834	959.8389
Trip distance (in miles)	London	471,877	4.6594
	Dublin	456,834	4.3947
Trip fare (in US$)	London	471,877	17.8833
	Dublin	456,834	17.6381
Surge multiplier	London	471,877	1.0755
	Dublin	456,834	1.0001
Estimated time of arrival	London	471,877	204.3132
(in seconds)	Dublin	456,834	252.1905
Driver experience (no. of trips)	London	471,877	1927.8160
	Dublin	456,834	397.9217
Rider experience (no. of trips)	London	471,877	94.5536
	Dublin	456,834	60.4299
Rating (1–5 stars)	London	314,255	4.6961
	Dublin	303,318	4.7169
Fraction of hard brakes	London	240,890	0.0823
	Dublin	215,462	0.0960
Fraction of hard acceleration	London	183,678	0.0560
	Dublin	164,016	0.0607
Fraction of hard brake over 0.2	London	240,890	0.1243
	Dublin	215,462	0.1727
Fraction of hard acceleration	London	183,678	0.0676
over 0.2	Dublin	164,016	0.0851

NOTE: N = number of observations.
SOURCE: Uber Technologies.

that since London has more drivers, they may be closer to the rider than drivers in Dublin. Both riders and drivers are also more experienced on the Uber app platform in London, indicating that it is an important control variable in the regression analysis, as Londoners are more likely to use the service.

Indicators of the relationship of population to driver parameters are presented in Table 2.3, such as the population to Uber driver ratio for both cities. The table shows the city's total population in 2016, and it is divided by the total number of Uber drivers in the period 2013–2016 (controlling for attrition) for each city. The ratio of the population to Uber drivers in Dublin is more than twice that of Uber drivers in London. This is in line with expectations given the more stringent entry regime in Dublin.

Table 2.3 Estimates of Driver to Population Ratio

	London	Dublin
Total number of licensed drivers who use the Uber app (2013–2016)	61,892	1,609
Population (2016, in millions)	8.79	1.331
Proportion of population to driver	142	827

SOURCE: For London: United Nations, World Population Prospects link, https://www.macrotrends.net/cities/22860/london/population (accessed May 9, 2022). For Dublin, Eurostat, https://www.macrotrends.net/cities/22860/london/population (accessed May 9, 2022). The value for drivers was obtained from Uber Technologies.

Lastly, Figure 2.1 shows how customer satisfaction with the rides compares in both cities. The figure includes data for all rated personal transportation trips completed in Dublin and London between November 2013 and December 2016. It presents the overall skewness of the ratings system toward five-star ratings, with the distribution of driver-quality ratings being relatively consistent across the two cities. As Figure 2.1 shows, quality ratings are highly right skewed, with nearly 81 percent of trips receiving a five-star rating using both Dublin and London. In contrast, less than 2 percent of trips receive one star. There seems to be no substantial difference in how customers rate their experience in Dublin and London. These results could indicate that the more intense training that ridesharing drivers are subjected to in Dublin does not translate to better customer evaluations, as one would expect.

Figure 2.1 Ratings Distribution on UberX Trips in Dublin and London (November 2013–December 2016)

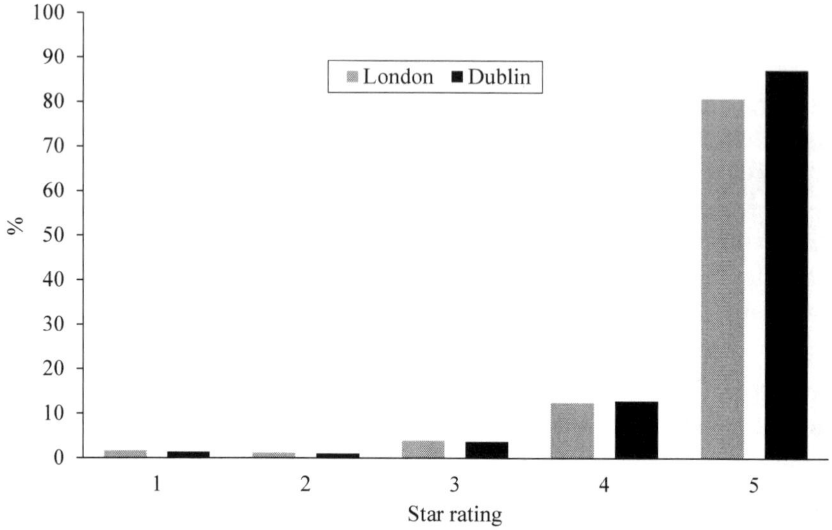

SOURCE: Uber Technologies.

Figure 2.2 shows the average per-mile fare in the two cities to relate to how the price of Uber ridesharing compares between the two cities. Between November 2013 and December 2016, the average base price (in U.S. dollars) was $5.58 per mile in Dublin, with a range of $3.00 to $10.00. In contrast, the average base price was $3.31 in London. The price range was $2.47 to $4.00 based on time and location. When surge pricing is considered, which is a measure of spot price based on supply and demand, the values in Dublin increase to a mean of $8.08, with a range of $4.16 to $25.00. The equivalent mean London prices are $5.81, with a range of $3.90 to $9.80. Using both methods of measuring base prices with and without the surge component used by Uber, the prices are higher in Dublin.

Figure 2.2 also shows the price effect analysis for the period 2013–2016. Initially, the London fare was higher, but fares in both cities converged in 2015, and then the London fares were lower throughout 2016 and stayed lower throughout the year. However, in the latest period, London prices were rising slightly; in contrast, Dublin fares have

Figure 2.2 Average Uber Fare (in US$) per Mile in Dublin and London (2013–2016)

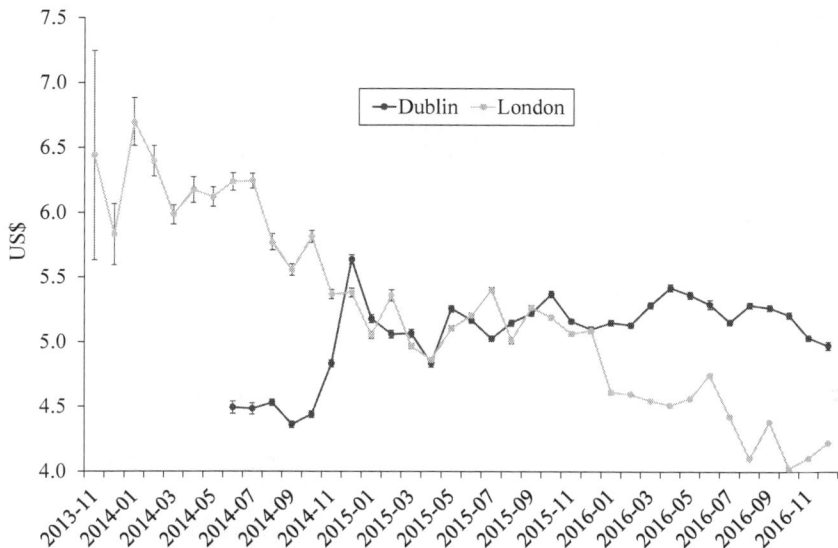

NOTE: The error bars are the 95 percent confidence intervals for the prices in both London and Dublin. The point estimate values are the averages of the fares per mile in the two cities.
SOURCE: Uber Technologies.

remained relatively stable (with some minor fluctuations). One explanation for the lower prices in London relates to the relatively higher supply of drivers compared to Dublin, and it is likely to be an outcome of the less stringent regulatory framework.

Measures of quality take various forms in different industries. In ridesharing, it is customer satisfaction and safety. If more relaxed occupational regulation has an influence on the quality of the ride, it is through these two outcomes. Where the ride takes place, however, is also an important determinant of both customer satisfaction and safety. Higher levels of congestion could be associated with greater customer frustration and an increased chance of a crash. Therefore, where the ride takes place within the city is a key variable in the analysis of the role for regulation in ridesharing. Uber hired MIT professor John Horton to develop the methodology for analysis—a grid based on the longitude and latitude of the place of the ride. Location dummies were generated by the algorithmic program package called TripMatchR. The program generates a map with numbers of observations in the form of a matrix, and then forms rectangular groups that have approximately the same total number of observations to generate the location of the ride. More specifically the TripMatchR algorithmically implements a geography-based clustering approach that partitions trip locales into "regions" or "clusters" by partitioning the trips into iso-counts. The approach has been used in other academic analysis of quality and demand for ride-sharing to control of location and time of ride (Hall et al. 2019; Hall, Horton, and Knoepel 2017).

Based on the estimates from the statistical model the results are consistent with the baseline graph that satisfaction is about 3 percentage points higher in the relatively more highly regulated Dublin than in London. The probabilities of getting a three-star and a five-star rating are according to Figure 2.1, about 4 percent for three-star ratings and about 81 percent for five-star ratings. If, for example, higher regulation reduces three-star ratings by 3 percentage points and increases the five-star ratings by 3 percentage points, the overall distribution would not change in any meaningful manner, since the five-star ratings occur with very high probability. However, when trip location is considered, the results suggest that London and Dublin have no significant difference on customer satisfaction.

The demand for taxi services is highly responsive to price and perceived safety of the ride. Any brake or acceleration on a trip with a force greater than 3.06 meters per second squared is considered a hard brake or hard acceleration, which is consistent with transportation industry standards (*Claims Journal* 2015). Both sets of telematics metrics are used because the distribution of the percentage of hard brakes or hard accelerations on trips could influence the proportion of trips that are identified as "safe" trips, using the 20 percent hard brakes or hard accelerations threshold. For example, the proportion of trips with greater than 20 percent hard brakes may differ significantly if hard-braking events tend to occur in relatively high or relatively low proportions on individual trips versus if hard-braking events tend to be relatively evenly distributed across trips. Importantly, hard braking has been shown to be one of the most important factors for predicting future crashes (*Claims Journal* 2015). Braking and acceleration events and the rates of braking and acceleration on individual trips are identified through the Uber app on a driver's smartphone. The estimates show that there is no difference between Dublin and London in the fraction of hard accelerations when the location of the trip is controlled for in the analysis. Moreover, the fractions of all rides where 20 percent or more of the accelerations are hard are not significantly lower in Dublin than in London when controlling for relevant factors.

The results show a higher probability of hard braking in Dublin, even controlling for base fare, trip distance (miles), trip duration (seconds), gender, driver experience (trips a driver conducted in their lifetime for Uber), rider experience (number of Uber trips of the rider who issued the rating), and time fixed effects. However, once the location effects are included in the model, there is no statistically significant difference between the two cities; that is, safety is not higher in the more regulated Dublin. Overall, the results suggest that the rides are no smoother in Dublin, where the intensity of regulation is higher than in London.

The key coefficients for each of the outcome variables by city discussed earlier that include customer satisfaction, hard accelerations, and hard braking are shown in Table 2.4. The estimates in the table present the influence of an observation in Dublin relative to London on measures of satisfaction, or corelates of safety such as hard accelerations or hard braking. The results for hard accelerations and braking are normalized by the fraction of all accelerations or braking during the trip. The coefficient values shown include controls such as trip distance, driver experience and their human capital, and the location of the trip.

Table 2.4 Coefficient Estimates and Standard Errors for Customer Satisfaction, Hard Accelerations, and Hard Braking for London versus Dublin (where Dublin is 1)

Outcome measure	Coefficient and standard errors
Customer satisfaction	−0.06
	(0.05)
Fraction of hard accelerations per trip	0.05
	(0.05)
Fraction of hard braking per trip	0.04
	(0.04)

SOURCE: Uber Technologies.

The results show no difference in these outcome measures if a trip was taken in London or Dublin.

CONCLUSIONS AND POTENTIAL PUBLIC POLICES

This chapter examines how variations in regulatory requirements affect quality outcomes. Specifically, the approach exploits how the differences in the stringency of becoming a licensed driver offering ride-sharing services in London and Dublin affect one measure of perceived quality (customer satisfaction) and two safety measures (hard accelerations and hard braking) obtained from Uber using the drivers' app with controls for area of the city, time of the day, day of week, and week of the year. Each of these locales has different levels of stringency for obtaining an occupational license, with barriers to entry being higher in Dublin. The analysis further describes and explores service availability and prices as value-added measures of quality. The approach allows for the examination of the role of regulation when one area (London) provides a more relaxed form of occupational regulation relative to another one (Dublin).

The results suggest that Uber service availability as measured by the Uber driver to population ratio is higher in London and prices are lower. These findings are not surprising since one would expect higher supply of Uber ridesharing services to be associated with lower prices, given Uber's market-driven approach toward ridesharing. Further, customer ratings are only slightly higher in the more stringently regulated Dublin and, when controlling for location of the ride, the difference is not statistically significant, which suggests that higher barriers do not seem to be correlated with customer satisfaction.

The results for safety measures show a higher percentage of trips with hard braking in Dublin, and this relationship ceases to be statistically significant when there are controls for location of the trip. In the empirical analysis across different specifications and statistical models regarding hard accelerations, the results also show that users have no higher-rated rides in Dublin, where the regulations are more stringent when controls for the location of the trip are considered. Based on these two safety indicators, there seems to be no justification for the considerably higher hurdles that ridesharing drivers must pass to legally operate in Dublin.

Overall, we find little evidence for greater regulatory constraints (at least of the type observed in these two jurisdictions) on ridesharing drivers. Further, the technological context for taxi and ridesharing driving is considerably different from when the regulatory provisions for taxi drivers were initially developed and physical maps were used for navigation. GPS technology, for example, provides drivers with detailed route information as well as information on traffic congestion, enabling them to conduct more efficient trips. The same technology is available to customers, so information asymmetry is lower. Consequently, it is questionable whether regulations with detailed topographical knowledge are as relevant as they used to be. Technologies that allow customers to rate their trips and the driver can mitigate problems associated with experience goods by ensuring that service standards are maintained. The broad conclusion from the assessment in this chapter is that the regulations of the taxi and ridesharing driving occupations should be changed to allow easier entry into the occupation. The relaxation of occupational licensing in this sector could lead to lower prices without any evidence that it would reduce customer satisfaction or the safety of the ride.

Notes

1. Uber has agreed to provide the data it collects through its app to address the research questions in this study. There were no incentives for Uber to provide data that might skew the data or results, since they were unaware of the approach or methods prior to providing the data.
2. These requirements are set out in the Taxi Regulation Act 2013 and the Taxi Regulation (Small Public Service Vehicle) Regulations 2015 (see www.irishstatute book.ie for all legal texts).
3. Author's own calculations based on information from the National Transport Authority available at https://www.nationaltransport.ie/taxi-and-bus-licensing/taxi/spsv-driver-licensing/apply-for-an-spsv-driver-licence-2/ (accessed June 22, 2022).
4. See data tables link here: https://www.gov.uk/government/statistics/taxi-and-private-hire-vehicles-statistics-england-2015, Table 'Taxi0101' (accessed June 22, 2022).
5. Private-hire vehicles are only permitted to pick up prearranged bookings and are not permitted to pick people up from the curb side. Taxis (also known as London black cabs) are licensed to pick people up from the curb side, i.e., hailing a cab.

6. https://tfl.gov.uk/info-for/taxis-and-private-hire/licensing/private-hire-driver
-licence (accessed June 22, 2022).
7. From all Uber data, observations from London and Dublin were selected if they
have rating and telematics information (some observations do not have both).
The random sample for London was obtained using the simple random sampling
method with replacement by repeating the following steps 10 times: 1) generate
random numbers and assign them to each observation; 2) select a subset of these
observations for the final sample according to the population ratio between London and Dublin.
8. The specific data are available on the time and dates of pickups and drop-offs from
Uber. The data used had at least 1,000 pickups and drop-offs for every time and
day and several thousand for peak periods.
9. The algorithm developed by Horton uses Python as its engine to generate a map
with number of observations in a form of matrix, and then forms rectangular
groups that have approximately the same total number of observations in the
matrix using the TripMatchR program (Horton 2016).
10. There was one outlier in Dublin, likely due to a coding error, which increases the
standard errors, and deleting it has little impact on the other variables.

References

Barrett, Sean D. 2003. "Regulatory Capture, Property Rights and Taxi Deregu-
lation: A Case Study." *Economic Affairs* 23(4): 34–40.
———. 2010. "The Sustained Impacts of Taxi Deregulation." *Economic
Affairs* 30(1): 61–65.
Beesley, Michael E. 1973. "Regulation of Taxis." *Economic Journal* 83(329):
150–172.
Cevero, R. 1985. "Safeguarding Suburban Mobility." *Transportation Research
Record* 1079: 16–23.
Claims Journal. 2015. "Hard Braking Most Likely Predictor of Future
Crashes: Progressive Data." May 19. https://www.claimsjournal.com/news/
national/2015/05/19/263424.htm (accessed December 13, 2021).
Dempsey, Paul Stephen. 1996. "Taxi Industry Regulation, Deregulation and
Reregulation: The Paradox of Market Failure." *Transport Law Journal*
24(1): 73–120.
DMR Statistics. 2017. "Uber Statistics, User Counts, Facts & News." http://
expandedramblings.com/index.php/uber-statistics/ (accessed June 28, 2017).
Financial Times. 2017. "How Uber and London Ended Up in a Taxi War."
September 27.
Hall, Jonathan, Jason Hicks, Morris M. Kleiner, and Rob Solomon. 2019.
"Occupational Licensing of Uber Drivers." Stanford, CA: Stanford Institute
for Theoretical Economics.

Hall, Jonathan, John Horton, and Daniel Knoepel. 2017. "Labor Market Equilibration: Evidence from Uber." Working paper. San Francisco: Uber Technologies.

Horton, John J. 2016. "TripMatchR" Version 1.0. http://john-joseph-horton.com/software/ (accessed December 13, 2021).

Huang, Wan-Ting, Chih-His Chang, Yu-Fen Hsu, and Jen-Hsiang Chuang. 2015. "Prognostic Factors for Mortality in Patients Hospitalized with Influenza Complications, in Taiwan." *International Health* 7(1): 73–75.

Katz, Lawrence F., and Alan B. Krueger. 2016. "The Rise and Nature of Alternative Work Arrangements in the United States, 1995–2015." Working Paper No. w22667. Cambridge, MA: National Bureau of Economic Research.

———. 2019. "The Rise and Nature of Alternative Work Arrangements in the United States, 1995–2015." ILR Review 72(2): 382–416.

Kleiner, Morris M. 2006. *Licensing Occupations: Ensuring Quality or Restricting Competition?* Kalamazoo, MI: W.E. Upjohn Institute for Employment Research.

———. 2015. *Guild-Ridden Labor Markets: The Curious Case of Occupational Licensing.* Kalamazoo, MI: W.E. Upjohn Institute for Employment Research.

Kleiner, Morris M., and Alan B. Krueger. 2010. "The Prevalence and Effects of Occupational Licensing." *British Journal of Industrial Relations* 48(4): 676–687.

———. 2013. "Analyzing the Extent and Influence of Occupational Licensing on the Labor Market." *Journal of Labor Economics* 31(2): S173–202.

Koumenta, Maria, and Mario Pagliero. 2016. *Measuring Prevalence and Labour Market Impacts of Occupational Regulation in the EU.* European Commission Report. Brussels: European Commission.

Rojeck, Miłosz, and Michał Masior. 2016. *The Effects of Reforms Liberalising Professional Requirements in Poland, European Commission Report.* Warsaw: Warsaw School of Economics.

Satariano, Adam. 2018. "Uber Regains Its License to Operate in London, a Win for Its New C.E.O." *New York Times*, June 26. https://www.nytimes.com/2018/06/26/technology/uber-london.html (accessed December 13, 2021).

———. 2021. "Uber Drivers Are Entitled to Worker Benefits, a British Court Rules." *New York Times*, February 19. https://www.nytimes.com/2021/02/19/business/uber-drivers-britain.html (accessed December 13, 2021).

Schaller, Bruce. 2007. "Entry Controls in Taxi Regulation: Implications of US and Canadian Experience for Taxi Regulation and Deregulation." *Transport Policy* 14(6): 490–506.

Shleifer, Andrei. 2010. "Efficient Regulation." In *Regulation vs. Litigation:*

Perspectives from Economics and Law, Daniel Kessler, ed. Chicago: University of Chicago Press, pp. 27–43.

Szary, Wiktor. 2017. "London Commuters Surprised by Transport Threat to Stop Uber Service. *Wall Street Journal.* https://www.wsj.com/articles/london-commuters-surprised-by-transport-threat-to-stop-uber-service-1506102210 (accessed June 21, 2022).

Teal, Roger F., and Mary Berglund. 1987. "The Impacts of Taxicab Deregulation in the USA." *Journal of Transport Economics and Policy* 21(1): 37–56.

Appendix 2A

Table 2A.1 Variable Descriptions of the Data from Uber

Variable	Description
City	Indicator for city, 0 = London and 1 = Dublin
Trip duration	Time spent for the driver to provide service from the departure location to destination, in seconds
Trip distance	Distance travelled for providing the service from the departure location to destination, in miles
Client fare	Amount charged for the given service, in US$
Driver experience	Number of trips that the driver provided on the Uber platform until the time he/she provided the current service
Gender	Gender of the driver, 0 = Female and 1 = Male
Surge pricing	An algorithmic technique that Uber used when there is a demand-supply imbalance to determine fares. Usually, the company raises the price of its offering if there is an increase in demand.
Rider experience	Number of trips that the rider received on the Uber platform until the time he/she provided the current service
Month	Thirty-seven dummy variables for each month between November 2013 and December 2016.
Day of week	Six dummy variables for day of the week, i.e., for Monday through Sunday.
Hour	Twenty-three dummy variables for hour of the day.
Begin trip cluster	Dummy variables generated by R package (TripMatchR) developed by Dr. John Horton of MIT that generates 1,023 Boolean variables that indicate geographical clusters for the pickup and drop-off locations. see Horton (2016).
End trip cluster	Boolean variables that indicate geographical clusters for the pickup and drop-off locations. see Horton (2016).

3
Tougher Licensing Requirements and Quality Outcomes

Driving Instructors in the United Kingdom

Maria Koumenta
Queen Mary, University of London and
Knee Center for the Study of Occupational Regulation

Mark Williams
Queen Mary, University of London

The driving instructor profession is regulated in most countries based on road safety and consumer protection against accidents and fatalities. However, the regulations and criteria are inconsistent across Europe. The U.K., for example, has one of the least restrictive regimes for becoming a driving instructor. Although there are stipulations regarding the type of training required, the corresponding exams, and subsequent testing for competence, there are no preconditions regarding primary or secondary education, the length of required training, or mandatory traineeship. This is in sharp contrast with some European counterparts, where a postsecondary education is often required (such as in Finland, Greece, and Romania), as well as lengthy training provisions (e.g., 300 hours in Belgium; 630 hours in France; two years in Estonia, Greece, and Ireland). This cross-country variation raises questions about whether higher levels of licensing stringency are correlated with better safety outcomes for road users.

The first initiative to formalize eligibility to teach individuals driving skills in the U.K. came in the late 1950s from the Motor Schools Association and the Royal Automobile Club (both independent associations formed by owners of driving schools). The register of approved driving instructors (ADIs) was accepted by the U.K. Parliament in 1964, and in 1970 membership of the register became compulsory, meaning that any person giving paid instruction to drive a motor car whose name is not on the register is guilty of an offense. Thus, in occupational regulation terms, driving instructors in the U.K. are licensed. As we show in the next section, however, a dual market of fully trained (licensed) and trainee driving (in the process of becoming licensed) instructors was in operation, both of which were eligible to provide driver teaching.

More recently, there have been changes involving the tightening of licensing requirements and the de facto abolition of the dual market for driving instruction. In this chapter we assess the impact of these proposals on the quality of the instructors and the service provided. In particular, we examine whether stricter licensing regulations imposed on driving instructors have resulted in better-quality providers operating in the market and better outcomes for learners as measured by their success in various aspects of the driving test. Empirically this is achieved by comparing such outcomes before and after the reforms took place.

REGULATORY CONTEXT

The Driver and Vehicle Standards Agency is the U.K. regulatory body that manages the register of licensed driving instructors. To qualify, applicants must pass a criminal record check, followed by success in a three-part test administered by the agency:

- Part 1: a computer-based driving/instructional theory and hazard perception test
- Part 2: a practical driving ability test
- Part 3: a practical instructional ability test

After candidates pass the first two tests, they can then apply to the regulatory body for a trainee license, which allows them to give paid driving instruction without supervision by a licensed instructor before taking the Part 3 qualifying test. The cost of taking all the required tests, obtaining a trainee license, and joining the ADI Register is approximately $1,030, of which about $150 goes toward the cost of the Part 3 test (i.e., the cost of moving from a trainee to an ADI). Registration is for four years, after which there is a renewal application. The total fee covers the issue of the ADI license and other administration costs, the cost of the check test, and a further Disclosure and Barring Service check prior to renewing their license at the end of the four-year period.

Only certified ADIs or potential ADIs who have been granted a trainee license by the regulator (hereafter "trainee instructor") can give paid, in-car driving instruction. In practice, the driving instructor profession in the U.K. operates as a dual market of certified ADIs (fully qualified to provide instruction), and partially qualified (trainee) driving instructors also legally allowed to give instruction. The difference between the two is that the former have passed Part 3 of the test, whereas the latter have only passed Parts 1 and 2. Therefore, in theory, it is left to the consumer to choose between the two service providers. Although instructors are legally required to inform the students of their status (through displaying their badge when they are giving instruction), anecdotal evidence collected by the Driver and Vehicle Licensing Agency showed that learners tend not to be aware of whether they are receiving instruction from a fully approved (ADI) or a trainee instructor, and the fee they were paying was often the same regardless of the instructor's status.

THE REFORM PROPOSALS

In 2013, the U.K. government reviewed the regulatory framework for driving instructors. Concerns were raised regarding the extent to which, after qualifying as fully approved instructor, individuals started deviating from the guidance provided by the Driver and Vehicle Licensing Agency. For this reason, in 2014 a new "standards check" was introduced that requires ADIs to undergo further assessment of their instructional methods at least once during the four-year period that their license is valid; otherwise, they risk being dropped from the register. The process involves an assessor observing and grading the ADI; the grade range is A (indicating a high standard of driving instruction), B (sufficient level of competence), or Fail (unsatisfactory driving instruction performance). The new system was largely seen as a tightening of the right-to-practice regulations in the industry.

Additional concerns emerged regarding the low completion rates among trainee driving instructors as evidenced by the large proportion of individuals who had completed the minimum required training (i.e., Parts 1 and 2) but had not progressed to complete the process (i.e., Part 3) and become ADIs. There was also evidence of high failure rates among those trainee instructors in the Part 3 test on instructional ability, despite multiple attempts. As a result, the market was populated by a mix of fully trained instructors and trainees (many with questionable ability to ever qualify), both of which could offer identical services and often at a similar price. Overall, this regime was seen to be compromising the quality of instruction received by prospective drivers, disincentivising trainee driving instructors from fully qualifying, and not providing transparency to the public, thus driving down standards in the market. As a result, the government put forward proposals to reform the trainee license scheme. In addition to improvements in the qualification tests, the proposals stipulated that trainee license holders cannot provide driving lessons for money unless they are accompanied by a fully licensed ADI for at least part of the duration of the total instruction.

RELEVANT LITERATURE

There is a marked absence of studies on the regulation of driving instructors and its impact on quality. One exception is a study on the deregulation of Portuguese driving schools in the late 1990s (Seim and Vitorino 2011). Prior to the reform, driving schools were heavily regulated by the state. There were restrictions on the numbers of licenses issued based on population size and minimum distance requirements from competitors. Additionally, the state imposed fee caps on the schools' pricing. These regulations were partially lifted in 1998, and preliminary results show that it had a direct impact on service availability as evidenced by a 116 percent increase in the number of driving schools by 2010. Avrillier, Hivert, and Kramarz (2010) explore the effect of a demand shock (the end of conscription in France, which automatically provided young French men with a driving license) on the heavily regulated French driving school industry. Their results demonstrate that as a result of the rigid entry restrictions (which included a long and costly path to become an instructor), the industry could not respond by quickly increasing supply (as it would have done if it was competitive), and therefore service availability suffered. The authors also find an increase in the price of driving lessons (even when the industry finally started growing) and a reduction in the number of individuals getting their licenses (which can be attributed to either better screening of low-skilled students or a deterioration of the quality of instruction offered by driving instructors).

Turning to the wider literature, we find some studies that parallel the rationale and quality measures proposed here. Several studies have examined the relationship between regulation stringency within the teaching profession and its effect on quality, using student test scores as an indicator of the latter. We deem these to be of interest, given that driving instructors are also engaged in a form of teaching. An early study by Kleiner and Petree (1988) examines the impact of variations in the restrictiveness of licensing on educational performance using state-level data for the 1972–1982 period. Their measures of performance include the average level of the SAT and ACT standardized test scores and the proportion of students who graduate high school; their results are mixed and dependent on the estimation technique. With regard to the standardized scores, the authors find a positive relationship between regulation and standardized test scores, while the reverse is true for graduation rates. In a similar vein, Angrist and Guryan (2004) study the relationship between testing prospective teachers (to certify they meet minimum standards) and subsequent performance by students. Their evidence is also mixed in that while students of accredited teachers do better on the Praxis test, teacher testing has a negative effect on the average SAT score of a teacher's undergraduate institution. Kane, Rockoff, and Staiger (2005) also find little difference in student achievement between students taught by licensed, unlicensed, and certified teachers in the same schools in New York, while Kane and Staiger (2005), using a quality measure based on improvements in student achievement, again find no evidence that licensed teachers are more effective.

DATA AND METHODOLOGY

The Department of Transport and the Driver and Vehicle Licensing Agency produce publicly available data on driving test pass rates for students and instructors that are on the U.K. government's website in a series of Excel files. The raw files are not organized in a consistent manner by geographical and time units. To remedy this, we aggregate the geographical units up to postcode level, maximizing the number of observations within panels. We are thus left with a data set of observations (time points) nested within U.K. postcode areas.

Within these files, we extract four measures of quality relating to the instruction and service. First, driving instructor quality within postcode by time cells is proxied by driving instructor practical test pass rates (Part 2 test). Second, quality of service is proxied by practical driving test pass rates of students. This is supplemented with two more indicators of service quality: practical test pass rates at first attempt and practical test pass rates at the first attempt with zero faults (a perfect test score).

Our goals in this chapter are as follows. First, we want to establish whether the reforms affected the quality of instructors as measured by their success in the Part 2 test. The reforms would have had a positive effect on the quality of instructors if it deterred those with substandard skills from entering the occupation. As such, we would expect to see an increase in the pass rates of instructors in the Part 2 test. Second, using the three indicators of learner outcomes (practical driving test pass rates, pass at first attempt, and pass at first attempt with zero faults), we examine whether the quality of service changed after the reform. Our analytical approach follows similar studies on the impact of licensing on teachers where teacher quality is derived from variables relating to student performance in relevant tests (see section on related literature). Third, we examine whether the reforms discouraged substandard trainee instructors from entering the occupation and/or encouraged them to exit it, as well as whether it incentivized trainees to take the tests so that they can fully qualify as fully licensed trainers (i.e., to switch from trainees to ADIs). In the final part of our analysis, we use price data from the U.K. Office for National Statistics to estimate changes in the cost of driving lessons.

The analysis examines descriptive trends in the numbers of trainees and fully qualified instructors over time and descriptive trends in several quality indicators, particularly before and after the reform. We extend this by examining variation in trends pre- and postreform within postcode areas by whether postcode areas fell into the top, middle, or bottom tercile in terms of the share of instructors who were trainees prior to the reform. This is an especially informative analysis as we expect the reform to affect both instructor and learner outcomes through its effect on the ratio of trainees to fully qualified instructors. Finally, we test the robustness of the descriptive associations by controlling for other factors that can account for the observed trends.

RESULTS

We begin by describing key aggregate trends in the data, starting with the number of instructors (see Figure 3.1). As can be seen, over time there has been a sharp decline in the number of trainee instructors

Figure 3.1 Number of Qualified and Trainee Driving Instructors over Time

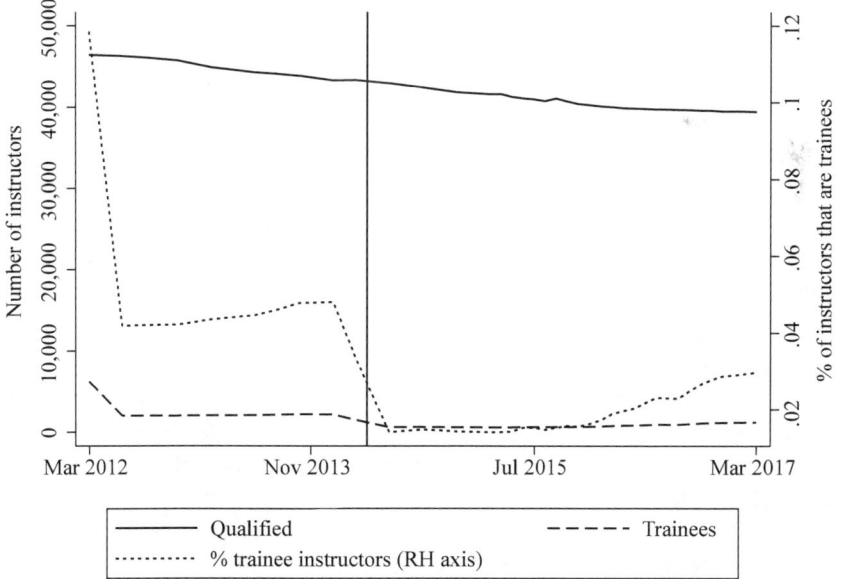

SOURCE: Authors' calculations using data from the Department of Transport and the Driver and Vehicle Licensing Agency.

and a smaller decline of qualified instructors (ADIs). Overall, the number of trainees is much smaller than the number of qualified instructors. The proportion of instructors who are trainees has fallen relatively dramatically, from around 12 percent in March 2012 to around 3 percent in March 2017. Examining the timing of the decline, it appears there were some anticipatory effects of the reform proposals (which became operational in April 2014). It is possible, for example, that trainee instructors who did not feel competent enough to pass the Part 3 exam and qualify as ADIs exited the market, leaving only the more competent ones active. Unfortunately, the data do not go back further in time, so we are unable to provide a longer-term picture to put this decline into context. Nonetheless, on the surface, the reform proposals have influenced the composition of instructors, which translates to fewer driving instructors in the market.

Turning to trends in the indicators of instructor quality, there was a 4 percentage point increase in the pass rate of trainee instructors in Part 2 (the driving practical) between March 2012 and March 2017, indicating that the average quality of instructors (at least new entrants and as judged by their success in this exam) has been improving over time (Figure 3.2). The rate of upward trend in pass rates seemed to increase after April 2014 (see the fitted values that fit a quadratic trend term). One possible explanation is that in anticipation of the reform, which would make entry and operation in the market more stringent, the low-quality prospective driving instructors were discouraged from entering the occupation. Overall, we can rule out explanations relating to the exam becoming easier or simpler, or those relating to any improvements in the training and support prospective driving instructors received between the two periods, as we know that the procedure and requirements remained the same.

We examine trends in instructor pass rates by whether postcode areas fall into the bottom, middle, or top third of the distribution of shares in trainee instructors for the period prior to the reform (Figure 3.3). If the reform increased the average quality of trainee instructors (as measured by pass rates on the instructor practical tests), then we might see steeper increases in pass rates in those areas that initially had a higher share of trainee instructors (as their higher share in those areas would translate to higher pass rates). While we find definite differences in pass rates prior to the reform proposals, with pass rates being

Figure 3.2 Instructor Practical Test Pass Rates over Time

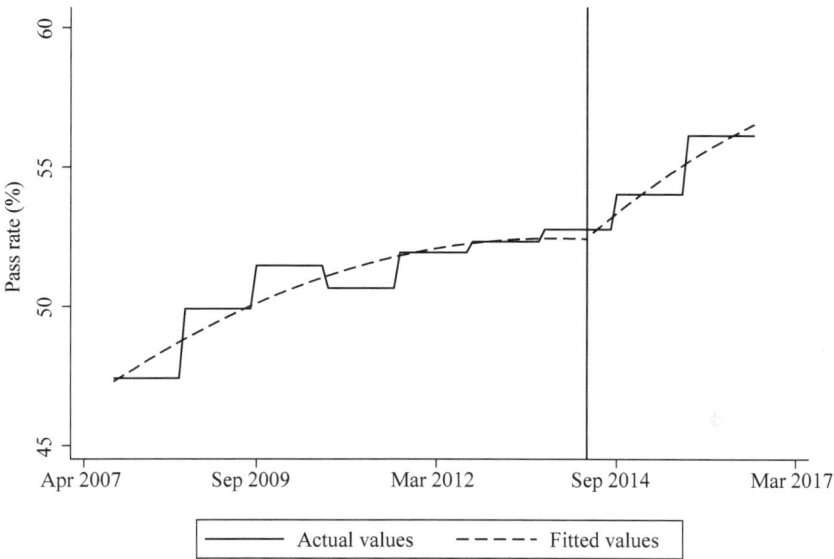

NOTE: Authors' calculations using data from the Department of Transport and the Driver and Vehicle Licensing Agency.

the lowest in areas with the highest share of trainee instructors, pass rates seem to improve the most in areas that had lower shares of trainee instructors to begin with.

Turning to our proxies for service quality for learners, before the reform, we observe a general upward trend in total practical test pass rates (Figure 3.4)—the part of the qualification process that is affected by driving instructors. After the reform, trends in practical test pass rates slowed and levelled out. By contrast, the theory test pass rates have been steadily falling, likely due in part to stricter standards imposed by the Driver and Vehicle Licensing Agency. Since the theory test must be taken before the practical test, the upward trend in practical pass rates may be due to elimination of very low ability would-be drivers who cannot pass the theory test as the procedures became stricter rather than an improvement in the quality of tuition received by would-be drivers. In Figure 3.5, we explore two more fine-grained measures of performance in the practical test: pass rates at first attempt (as learners

Figure 3.3 Instructor Practical Test Pass Rates—by Prereform Trainee Instructor Share Tercile

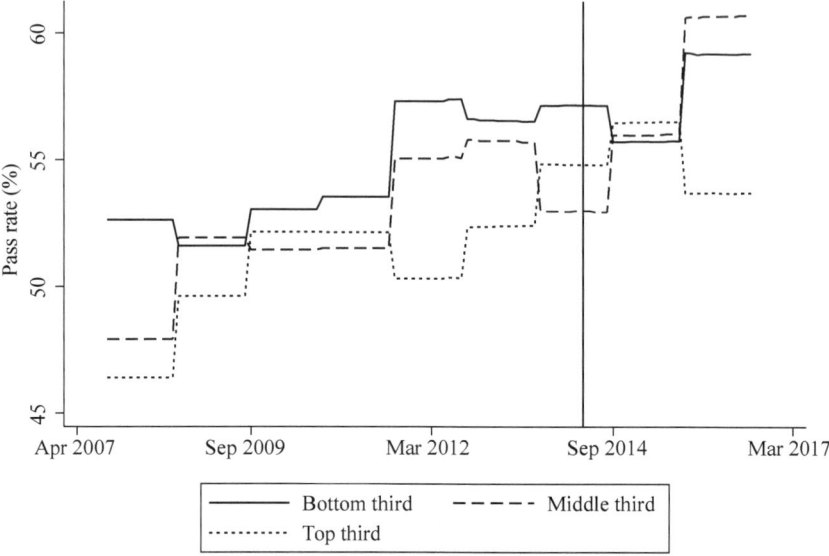

SOURCE: Authors' calculations using data from the Department of Transport and the Driver and Vehicle Licensing Agency.

can take the test multiple times if they fail) and zero-faults pass rates at first attempt (obtaining a perfect score on their first attempt). Here too we find similar trends as with the overall pass rates for the practical test: a general upward trend that levels out after the reform proposals. On the face of it, then, it appears the reform has had no visible effect on the quality of the service as measured by performance on the practical test by learners.

Finally, we explore whether trends in practical test pass rates vary over time according to the share of instructors who were trainees prior to the reform (Figure 3.6). While we find clear differences in pass rates according to the share of instructors who were trainees, with postcodes in the bottom third having significantly lower pass rates than all of the postcodes, we find trends that are broadly similar to those in Figure 3.4. Consequently, even in this more fine-grained approach, we find little evidence that the reform resulted in higher pass rates for learners.

Figure 3.4 Learner Practical and Theory Test Pass Rates

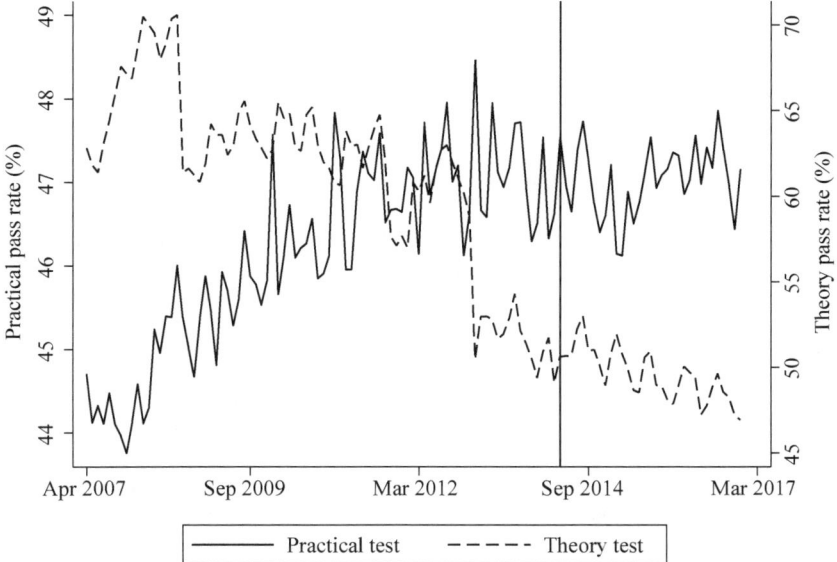

SOURCE: Authors' calculations using data from the Department of Transport and the Driver and Vehicle Licensing Agency.

Multivariate Estimates

Our analysis so far has been descriptive in nature. As such, it does not consider other factors that might account for the associations we observe in the previous graphs. We can improve on this approach by comparing each of the quality indicators before and after the reform, stripping out all the time-invariant factors that might affect the outcomes of interest.[1] In terms of exploring the effect of the reform on instructors, we examine four outcomes (which relate to our previous descriptive analysis):

1) The number of trainee instructors. This is a proxy for the number of people wanting to enter the profession as an ADI. If this decreased after the reform, it could signify that new and possibly lower-skilled individuals were discouraged from entering the profession or decided to exit because of concerns about their ability to qualify (i.e., pass the Part 3 test).

Figure 3.5 Learner Practical Test Pass Rates—First Attempt and Zero Faults

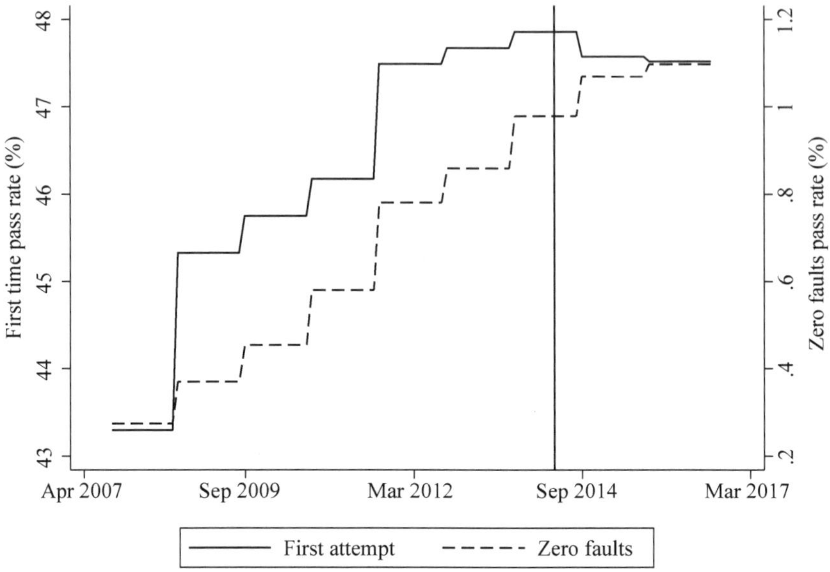

SOURCE: Authors' calculations using data from the Department of Transport and the Driver and Vehicle Licensing Agency.

2) The number of Part 3 tests taken. If these decrease, it could also signify discouraging new and low-quality entrants.[2]

3) The pass rate of instructors taking the practical test (defined as the percentage of passes over the number of tests taken). If the pass rate increases, it may signify an increase in quality of new instructors after the reform.

4) The number of qualified instructors before and after the reform proposals.

Starting with the estimates for instructor outcomes (Table 3.1), we find that the number of trainee instructors fell in the period following the reform proposals relative to before it (Column 1), and that this is robust to the general time trend (Column 2). This translates to roughly 78 percent fewer trainee instructors within postcodes on average in the period after the reforms. Nonetheless, the number of Part 3 tests being

Figure 3.6 Learner Practical Test Pass Rates by Prereform Trainee Instructor Share Tercile

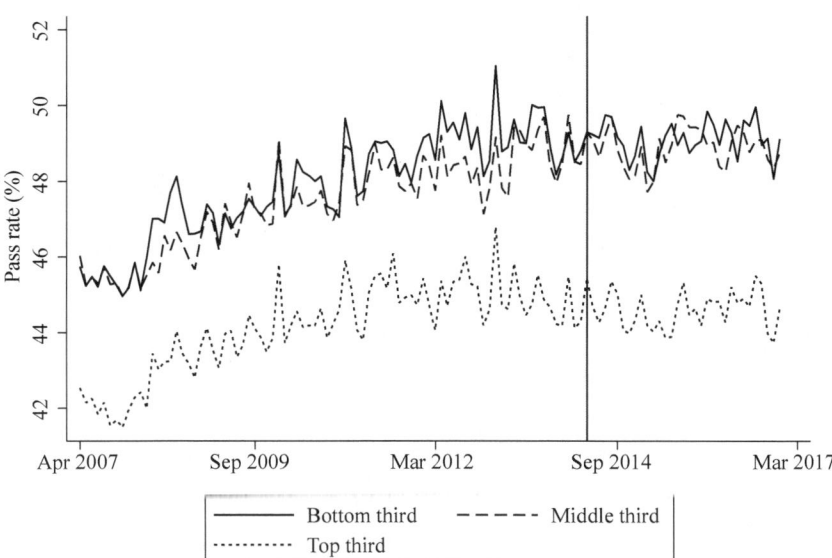

SOURCE: Authors' calculations using data from the Department of Transport and the Driver and Vehicle Licensing Agency.

taken appears to be higher than the general trend after the reform proposals once the time trend is taken into account (Column 4), while the pass rate of trainees was no different before and after the reform proposals once general time trends are taken into account (Column 6). Finally, the number of qualified instructors was lower after the reforms but only marginally—by roughly 1.7 percent (Column 8). Taken together, these results imply that more tests are being taken postreform than expected, but at the same time the number of instructors is falling despite the pass rate remaining stable, perhaps due to exiting.

We examine another four outcomes in terms of the effect on driving students. First, the number of practical tests taken by students. If this falls postreform, it may indicate a fall in the access to instructors, and so fewer people are taking the test within a given time period. Second, the pass rate of the practical test (defined as the percentage of passes over the number of tests taken). This is a straightforward indicator of

Table 3.1 Fixed-Effects Regression Models of Instructor Outcomes Pre- and Postreform

	(1)	(2)	(3)	(4)	(5)	(6)	(7)	(8)
	Number of trainee instructors (log)		Number of Part 3 tests (log)		Part 3 test pass rate		Number of qualified instructors (log)	
Pre vs. post period	−1.017***	−1.531***	−0.811***	0.260***	4.243***	−1.442	−0.112***	−0.017***
	(0.047)	(0.071)	(0.054)	(0.066)	(1.122)	(1.272)	(0.014)	(0.004)
Time trend		0.015***		−0.019***		0.102***		−0.003***
		(0.002)		(0.001)		(0.017)		(0.000)
Constant	2.485***	1.379***	4.680***	5.517***	52.561***	48.121***	5.483***	5.687***
	(0.034)	(0.138)	(0.014)	(0.047)	(0.280)	(0.856)	(0.010)	(0.039)
R^2	0.741	0.755	0.623	0.812	0.464	0.501	0.995	0.996
N obs	4,752	4,752	7,128	7,128	7,116	7,116	4,752	4,752
N panels	147	147	78	78	78	78	147	147

NOTE: *significant at the 0.05 level; **significant at the 0.01 level; ***significant at the 0.001 level. Robust standard errors clustered on postcode area in parentheses.

the quality of instruction. Third, the pass rate at first attempt. Fourth, the proportion of passes at the first attempt with zero faults (a perfect score). These latter two are also straightforward indicators of the quality of instruction.

Turning to the estimates for learner outcomes (Table 3.2), we examine the number of practical tests taken by students and find that there is no difference before and after the reforms (Column 1), but when we take into account the reduction in practical tests through the time trend, the number of tests taken is about 13 percent higher (Column 2). We also find higher pass rates after the reform than before it (Column 3), but once we consider the general upward trend in pass rates (as previously mentioned, perhaps this is due to the tightening up of the theory test procedures), we find the effect in fact becomes negative. There is a similar pattern of both higher pass rates at first attempt and zero faults at first attempt being higher in the period following the reform, but yet again, once we factor in the general time trends in these two outcomes, the pass rates in the period postreform become lower than before it. Overall, these improved estimates further confirm the robustness of our descriptive analysis.

PRICE OF DRIVING LESSONS

In the final part of our analysis, we use data from the U.K. Office for National Statistics to calculate the price of driving lessons (one hour) before and after the reform proposals. We present data on both the nominal price and the price adjusted for 2017 CPI. As Figure 3.7 shows, after a period of falling real prices, the price of driving lessons increased after the reform proposals. Although the price of a driving lesson at the cut-off date of the last available data is still lower than it was before the reform proposals, there is a clear upward trajectory. One possible explanation for this trend relates to the lower availability of driving instructors in the market after the reform proposals, which has enabled incumbents to increase their fees.

Table 3.2 Fixed-Effects Regression Estimates of Learner Outcomes Pre- and Postreform

	(1)	(2)	(3)	(4)	(5)	(6)	(7)	(8)
	Number of practical tests taken		Test pass rates		Practical tests pass rate (first attempt)		Practical test pass rates (zero faults)	
Pre *vs.* post period	−0.009	0.127***	1.283***	−1.147***	1.752***	−1.533***	0.535***	−0.032
	(0.022)	(0.020)	(0.269)	(0.263)	(0.257)	(0.234)	(0.043)	(0.046)
Time trend		−0.002***		0.042***		0.061***		0.011***
		(0.000)		(0.005)		(0.005)		(0.001)
Constant	6.766***	6.866***	47.888***	46.107***	47.189***	44.426***	0.647***	0.170**
	(0.006)	(0.017)	(0.073)	(0.240)	(0.066)	(0.286)	(0.011)	(0.052)
R^2	0.906	0.909	0.744	0.763	0.835	0.875	0.638	0.729
N obs.	13,412	13,412	13,400	13,400	12,396	12,396	12,396	12,396
N panels	116	116	116	116	116	116	116	116

NOTE: *significant at the 0.05 level; **significant at the 0.01 level; ***significant at the 0.001 level. Robust standard errors clustered on postcode area in parentheses.

Figure 3.7 Prices for One-Hour Driving Lessons

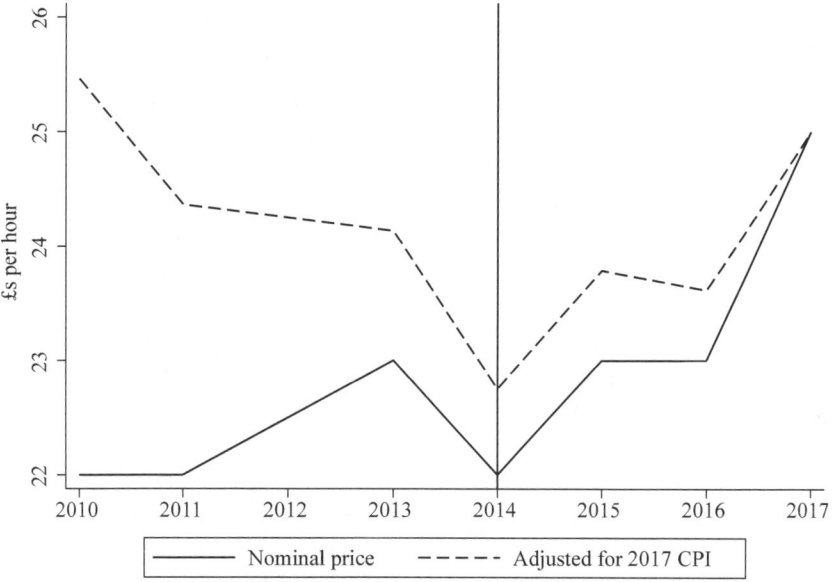

SOURCE: Authors' calculations using Office for National Statistics data.

CONCLUSION

Entry into the profession of driving instructor in the U.K. has been subject to compulsory training requirements, although in practice there was a dual market of fully trained and trainee driving instructors who both could offer instruction for payment. This study aimed to explore the impact of the proposals to reform the driving instructor occupation in the U.K. In particular, the state was concerned that the quality of instruction offered to prospective drivers was compromised because trainee driving instructors often were not able to finish their training and therefore may be unable to provide the same quality instruction as fully licensed instructors. The 2014 reform initiatives were designed to increase the stringency of regulations such that only ADIs or trainees accompanied by ADIs would be able to offer paid tuition. In addition, the U.K. made the requirements to demonstrate continuing professional competence more strict. In this study, we assess the effect that the proposed changes had on the quality of service.

Starting with service availability, we looked at various outcomes for instructors. Our results show that the number of trainee instructors fell in the period following the reform proposals relative to before, with around 78 percent fewer trainee instructors within postcodes on average in the period after. There was also a small drop in the number of trainee driving instructors qualifying as ADIs. We interpret this as a sign that the reform proposals discouraged instructors in the labor market from continuing to practice (e.g., those that had previously failed the Part 3 test) or from entering the market in the first place. In that sense, the reform proposals meet their goals. However, the question is whether this reduced availability of driving instructors in the market (which can be adverse for consumers) translated to any benefits for the other quality indicators.

The reform proposals also seem to have put some pressure on trainee instructors to take the relevant tests so they could qualify (as the reform proposals intended), but we do not observe an improvement in the Part 3 test pass rates before and after. As such, we find no evidence of improvement in the quality of instructors. Turning to the outcomes for learners, we note that in addition to the proposed restrictions on the ability of trainee instructors to provide fully unsupervised instruction, we have the parallel improvements in the standards check (i.e., the review of instructional methods that happens once every four years), both of which were intended to affect the quality of instruction offered. Overall, we do not find any improvement in the three quality measures of learner performance. If anything, overall pass rates, pass rates at first attempt, and zero faults all become negative (once time trends are considered). Why these measures deteriorate is an open question, but our broad conclusion is that the reform proposals are certainly not showing an improvement in the quality of driving students as we had expected.

Our final measures of quality relate to prices. We find that the price of a one-hour lesson increased after the reform proposals. This is in line with expectations relating to how the lower supply of practitioners in the market is likely to affect the cost of these services. Given that the state does not specify a minimum number of driving lessons learners have to do before taking the driving test, it is possible that the trend of increasing prices we observe is affecting demand for driving lessons.

To conclude, the reform proposals attempted to make access to the driving instructor occupation more stringent. From the evidence presented here, it is doubtful whether this has resulted in better quality outcomes. Our findings echo other studies that have on average failed to show that more intense driver education courses produce safer drivers. A recent review of international data on accidents by the U.S. Department of Transportation (2009), for example, concludes that there is little evidence that the crash records of those who underwent intensive formal training are different from those who did not. Instead, according to the report, traffic management, attitudes, motivations, peer influences, and cognitive and decision-making skills are more influential in shaping driving behaviors (see also Abdel-Aty and Radwan [2000]; French et al. [1993]; and Sümer [2003] for further evidence). While a detailed analysis of this body of work is beyond the scope of this study, the findings have led many to question what should be expected of driving instructors and the stringency of the level of training to which they should be subject in order to meet such expectations (Waller 1978). A key contribution of our analysis to such policy debates is to show that service quality in the market for driving instruction does not change much with more stringent entry criteria. The fact that we find no evidence that increasing the hurdles to become licensed is associated with better outcomes deserves attention from policymakers in highly regulated jurisdictions. Overall, we think that the findings from this chapter make a contribution to these wider debates about the optimal level of regulation of driving instructors.

Notes

1. This empirical strategy is known as fixed effects regression models in econometrics.
2. As before, we do not expect this to be affected by the cost of the Part 3 exam (i.e., £111 of a total of £750).

References

Abdel-Aty, Mohamed, and A. Essam Radwan. 2000. "Modelling Traffic Accident Occurrence and Involvement." *Accident Analysis & Prevention* 32(5): 633–642.

Angrist, Joshua D., and Jonathan Guryan. 2004. "Teacher Testing, Teacher Education, and Teacher Characteristics." *American Economic Review* 94(2): 241–246.

Avrillier, Paul, Laurent Hivert, and Francis Kramarz. 2010. "Driven Out of Employment? The Impact of the Abolition of National Service on Driving Schools and Aspiring Drivers." *British Journal of Industrial Relations* 48(4): 784–807.

French, Davina J., R.J. West, James Elander, and John Martin Wilding. 1993. "Decision-Making Style, Driving Style, and Self-Reported Involvement in Road Traffic Accidents." *Ergonomics* 36(6): 627–644.

Kane, Thomas J., and Douglas O. Staiger. 2005. "Using Imperfect Information to Identify Effective Teachers." Unpublished working paper. http://citeseerx.ist.psu.edu/viewdoc/download?doi=10.1.1.701.1105&rep=rep1&type=pdf (accessed December 14, 2021).

Kane, Thomas J., Jonah E. Rockoff, and Douglas O. Staiger. 2008. "What Does Certification Tell Us about Teacher Effectiveness? Evidence from New York City." *Economics of Education Review* 27(6): 615–631.

Kleiner, Morris M., and Daniel L. Petree. 1988. "Unionism and Licensing of Public School Teachers: Impact on Wages and Educational Output." In *When Public Sector Workers Unionize*, Richard B. Freeman and Casey Ichniowski, eds. Chicago: University of Chicago Press, pp. 305–322.

Seim, Katja, and Maria Ana Vitorino. 2011. "Efficiency Gains from Removing Entry and Price Controls: Evidence from a Change in Regulation." Wharton School Working Paper. Philadelphia: Wharton School, University of Pennsylvania.

Sümer, Nebi. 2003. "Personality and Behavioral Predictors of Traffic Accidents: Testing a Contextual Mediated Model." *Accident Analysis & Prevention* 35(6): 949–964.

U.S. Department of Transportation, National Highway Traffic Safety Administration. 2009. *Feasibility Study on Evaluating Driver Education Curriculum.* Washington, DC: U.S. Department of Transportation.

Waller, Patricia F. 1978. *Driver Performance Tests: Their Role and Potential.* Report No. DOT-HS-7-01698. Chapel Hill: University of North Carolina, Highway Safety Research Center.

4
Pharmacists in Italy

Eva Pagano
Mario Pagliero
Emanuele Pivetta
Lorenzo Richiardi
University of Turin

In Italy, as well as in many other countries, the work of pharmacists and the production, trade, and distribution of drugs is heavily regulated—justifiably so, considering the dangers associated with the improper use of medicines. Most drugs must be distributed through an authorized pharmacy, the main exception being over-the-counter (OTC) drugs, which are subject to lighter regulation. Pharmacies must employ licensed pharmacists, who are subject to educational requirements. The number of pharmacies and their locations are also subject to strict regulation, and they are established through an administrative procedure that links the number of pharmacies in a given city to the size of the local population. The rules used to determine the number of pharmacies in each city are relatively stable, although significant changes occurred in 1991 and 2012, which provided for increases in pharmacies.

Since the price of most drugs sold in Italian pharmacies (with the exception of OTC drugs) is also regulated, the key factor affecting the quality of the service is product accessibility. Therefore, this chapter focuses on the impact of regulation on the availability of pharmacies and its potential effects on human health. We use health outcomes measures from hospital admission records that can capture the potential impact of access to medicines (and the other services provided in pharmacies) on the health of the population.

INSTITUTIONAL CONTEXT: THE EUROPEAN
PHARMACY MARKET

The pharmacy market in Europe is characterized by significant government control on entry, scope of activities, and profit margins. After a series of reforms over the past two decades, the system began to change.

Vogler, Habimana, and Arts (2014) classify countries into two broad groups: regulated countries, such as Austria, Denmark, Finland, and Spain, and less-regulated countries, such as England, Ireland, the Netherlands, Norway, and Sweden.[1] In general, regulated countries apply demographic rules (e.g., number of potential consumers for each pharmacy) and geographic criteria (e.g., distance to existing pharmacies) to determine entry into the market. Moreover, they tend to impose restrictions on ownership of pharmacies. Less-regulated countries were subject to different types of liberalization.[2]

The authors find that after deregulation, the number of pharmacies increased and the number of inhabitants per pharmacy dropped. This phenomenon was particularly strong in Norway and Sweden. These new pharmacies tend to be established mainly in urban areas, with few new pharmacies in rural areas. There are indications of an increased workload for pharmacists in some deregulated countries. Moreover, they note that after liberalization, specific stakeholders, such as wholesalers, may gain market power and possibly limit competition (Norway), partially offsetting the increase in competition because of the larger number of pharmacies. Anell (2005) finds somewhat similar results in his study of the pharmacy market in Norway and Iceland—namely that the number of pharmacies increases (and prices tend to decrease), but also concentration seems to increase as a result of horizontal integration of formerly independent pharmacies.

Schaumans and Verboven (2008) study entry and conduct regulation of pharmacies and physicians in Belgium, where both professions have regulated fees and markups, and where there is a ban on most types of advertising. Moreover, there are significant restrictions to entry based on geography and size of the local population. The presence of these kinds of regulations is often justified to ensure a minimum availability of supply in less profitable regions without inducing excessive entry elsewhere. The authors evaluate this public interest motivation and develop a model of entry by two types of professions: physicians and pharmacists. The results show that entry in one profession has a positive effect on the profitability of entry into the other profession, supporting the idea that these professions are strategic complements. Moreover, geographical entry restrictions substantially limit the number of firms. They conclude that the current regime of highly regulated markups and restricted entry seems to protect the private interests of existing pharmacies more than the public interests. They also suggest that it is possible to induce a large shift in rents to consumers without reducing geographic coverage by combining reductions in geographical and markup restrictions.

The Italian Pharmacy Market

Pharmacists are entitled to distribute prescription drugs to consumers. They are required to meet educational requirements and pass a licensing exam. OTC drugs can be distributed to consumers within pharmacies, supermarkets, and other shops.[3] In the latter two cases, a pharmacist must always be present during store hours.[4] There is little variability in the type of service provided by Italian pharmacies, since prices are fixed and the training and skills of pharmacists are strictly regulated. Hence, the most important aspect of quality is the accessibility of pharmacies to consumers. This is particularly relevant in smaller towns and villages, namely in rural areas, where older consumers (or those affected by chronic pathologies) might have substantial mobility problems.

There are few studies on the Italian market for pharmacies. Calzolari et al. (2013) investigate how pharmacies adjust prices based on the composition of their consumers. They empirically study the pricing strategies of Italian pharmacies in the market for diapers and some hygiene products, whose prices are not regulated. The empirical estimation strategy exploits the demographic rule that links the number of pharmacies to the population size in each city (this approach will be described in detail below). The results show that more competitive markets tend to have significantly lower prices. Mocetti (2016) provides evidence that the possibility of inheriting the ownership of a pharmacy may affect the career choices of pharmacists' children and intergenerational mobility.

The Pharmacy Market and Public Health

Many studies over the past 40 years have assessed potential health effects of pharmacist-provided direct patient care services. There is substantial evidence that pharmacist involvement in direct patient care can have beneficial effects on patient health outcomes (Chisholm-Burns et al. 2010).

Because community pharmacists are among the most accessible health care providers, the clinical services they provide can have a major impact on patient health outcomes. Their access to prescription refill information and frequent interactions with patients uniquely position them to help patients adhere to a medicine regimen. This is evidenced especially in the treatments of Type 2 diabetes (Nazar et al. 2015; Pousinho et al. 2016), cardiovascular diseases (Altowaijri, Phillips, and Fitzsimmons 2013; Koshman et al. 2008; Tsuyuki et al. 2016), and seasonal influenza (Gai and Feng 2017; Kirkdale et al. 2017). However, as evidenced by the review of Blalock et al. (2013) in the United States, the effectiveness of pharmacist-provided direct patient care services delivered in the community setting is more limited than in other settings, such as hospitals. Only 50 of the 134 outcomes (37.3 percent) examined in the 21 articles that Blalock and colleagues reviewed revealed between-group differences or changes over time that were consistent with beneficial intervention effects.

Besides positive impact on health outcomes, density of community pharmacies is also associated with an increase in drug supply (mainly OTC medicines), some of which may be abused. Cooper (2013) identifies OTC medicine abuse in many countries together with a range of other problems. The first is the direct harm caused by the pharmacological or psychological effects of drug abuse or misuse. Although there was variability across countries, five key groups emerged: codeine-based (especially compound analgesic) medicines, cough products (particularly dextromethorphan), sedative antihistamines, decongestants, and laxatives. The second is the physiological harm related to the adverse effects of a secondary active ingredient in a compound formulation, causing, for example, upper gastrointestinal bleeding. Both types of harm led to concerns about overdoses and excessive use of emergency services. Finally, the literature identified other negative effects, such as progression to abuse of other substances, economic costs, and effects on personal and social life (Cooper 2013). To the best of our knowledge, the association between community pharmacy density and increased hospitalizations due to medicine abuse has not been systematically explored.

TYPE OF REGULATION

In Italy, most drugs must be distributed through an authorized pharmacy, the main exception being over the counter (OTC) drugs, which are subject to lighter regulation. The number of pharmacies and their location is subject to strict regulation determined through an administrative procedure. Each of the 20 Italian regional governments determines the number of pharmacies in each municipality and their exact location (minimum distance requirements between pharmacies also apply). The procedure is complex, and the process also involves city councils, local health services, and the professional associations of pharmacists. The size of the population living in each municipality is the main determinant of the number of pharmacies, and the function that maps the local population to the maximum number of pharmacies in each municipality is set by law. Since 1968, three such functions have been used.

The first, used between 1968 and 1991, required a maximum of one pharmacy every 5,000 inhabitants in municipalities with a population up to 25,000, and one pharmacy every 4,000 inhabitants in larger towns. In small municipalities, with populations below 25,000, if the remainder obtained dividing the population by 5,000 is larger than 2,500, it is possible to open an additional pharmacy. In larger towns, the remainder obtained after having assigned one pharmacy to every 4,000 inhabitants is ignored. This rather complex requirement generates the step function with somewhat irregular steps described in Figure 4.1.

The second function, in place between 1991 and 2012, required one pharmacy for every 5,000 inhabitants in municipalities up to 12,500, and one pharmacy for every 4,000 in larger towns. The remainder allows for the opening of a new pharmacy only if it is larger than 50 percent of the population requirement. Broadly speaking, this new function increases the number of pharmacies by decreasing the population threshold (12,500 instead of 25,000) and by not ignoring the remainders

Figure 4.1 Number of Pharmacies Allowed in Each Municipality According to the Demographic Rule

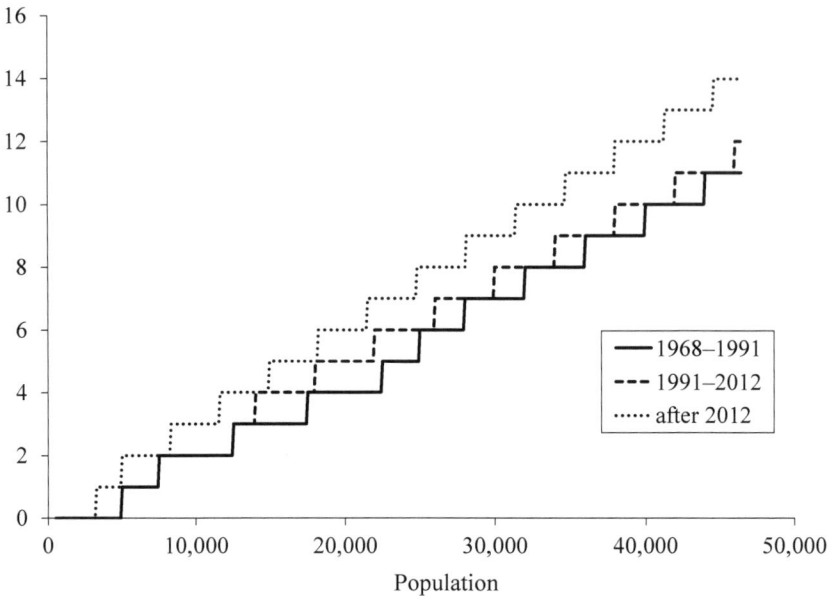

NOTE: The figure reports the number of pharmacies allowed to operate in each municipality as a function of the local population according to the demographic rule in place in three different periods.

SOURCE: Authors' calculations based on laws 475, 1968; 362, 1991; and 27, 2012.

in larger towns. Figure 4.1 compares this new step function with the one in place between 1968 and 1991.

The third function, introduced in 2012, provides for one pharmacy every 3,300 inhabitants. As before, the remainder allows for the opening of a new pharmacy only if it is larger than 50 percent of the population requirement. This change generates the third step function described in Figure 4.1. These new rules further increase the number of pharmacies. In principle, the demographic rules described in Figure 4.1 provide for a simple rule that links local population to number of pharmacies. However, a number of complications arise in the application of such rules, which make the link between number of pharmacies and population much more complex, as shown in Figure 4.2.

Figure 4.2 Number of Pharmacies and Population in Italian Municipalities

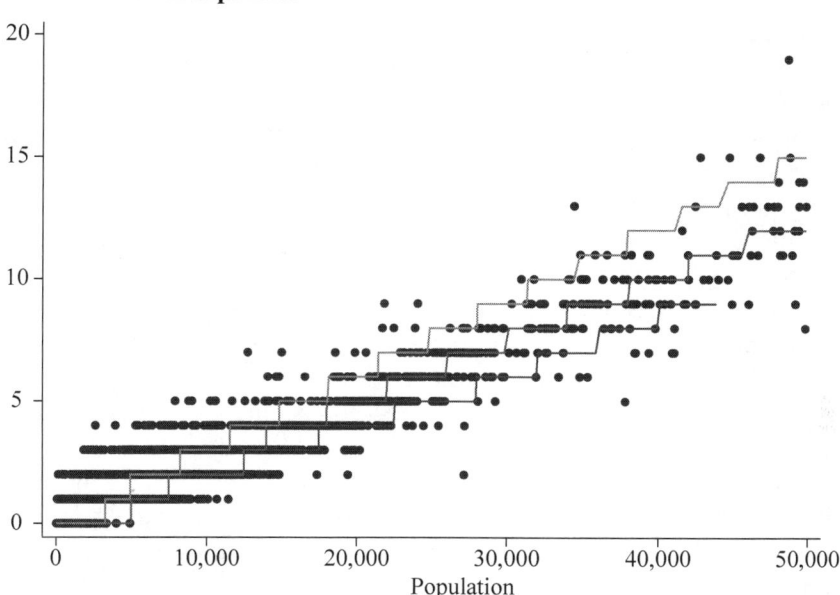

NOTE: The figure shows the number of pharmacies in each Italian municipality and the local population in 2015, with the three demographic rules used in the 1968–2016 period (see Figure 4.1).

SOURCE: Authors' calculations based on data from Istat and Italian Ministry of Health, and laws 475, 1968; 362, 1991; and 27, 2012.

The first issue relates to the municipalities with more pharmacies than the number set by the demographic rule. This may occur as a result of the status quo in 1968 or as a consequence of shrinking population in some municipalities. In absence of a clear indication of which pharmacy is supposed to close, and being generally profitable businesses, pharmacies in excess of the demographic rule are often allowed to operate. This allows for municipalities with more pharmacies than what the demographic rule would predict.

The second complication relates to small villages, which may not be entitled to a pharmacy according to the demographic rule. In rural areas, the closest pharmacy may prove to be too far away to guarantee a minimum availability of medicines. Therefore, exceptions to the rule are possible, and additional pharmacies can be allowed in small villages (less than 12,500 inhabitants) in rural areas (but subject to minimum distance requirements from other pharmacies).

A third concern arises as a consequence of the complex procedure required to update the list of pharmacies and then to select the pharmacists in charge of each pharmacy (this requires a public competition subject to specific rules). As a result, years of delay are not uncommon. Such an inefficient administrative procedure results in municipalities with fewer pharmacies than what the demographic rule would predict. In 2016, only a few regions had completed the procedures to update the list and opened the required new pharmacies (Bocci 2016). Finally, additional pharmacies may be opened (at most 5 percent of the total) in locations with large flows of people such as train stations, airports, and large shopping centers (but subject to specific minimum distance requirements from other pharmacies).

Each change in regulation was motivated by the desire to increase the availability of pharmacies. However, as described above, the impact was delayed because of slow implementation. The reforms took place during a period in which other attempts to liberalize some professional service markets also occurred. These were typically opposed by professional associations, and their effects were significantly attenuated with respect to the initial goals. The most significant example is the so-called Bersani reform in 2006, which canceled price floors (at the time still in place for a number of professions) and lifted the ban on commercial advertising and contingent fees. The market for OTC drugs was also liberalized, allowing supermarkets to enter into a highly regulated market, in direct competition with pharmacies (see Pagliero [2015] for a description of these reforms and some evidence on their impact).

QUALITY INDICATORS

As discussed above, pharmacists are considered primary health care providers—chronically ill patients often ask their pharmacists about their pathologies, medications, and other needs. For this reason, pharmacies represent an important factor contributing to the management of chronic diseases. Based on the organization of the Italian National Health Care system and clinical characteristics, and for reasons described below, we select four health outcomes of interest: 1) influenza and influenza-associated complications, including pneumonia; 2) diabetes; 3) acute coronary syndromes, including acute myocardial infarction (AMI); and 4) upper gastrointestinal bleeding.

Influenza

Influenza is characterized by seasonal outbreaks—at least one during the cold seasons—and its incidence and mortality depend on individual-related factors (e.g., age, comorbidities, immunocompetence), environmental factors (e.g., low temperatures, time course of the outbreak) and medical factors (e.g., antiviral treatment) (Huang et al. 2015). The World Health Organization suggests annual preventive vaccination, especially for high-risk populations (such as older people, pregnant women, or immunocompromised hosts). In these subgroups of the population, the risk of hospital admissions and death for influenza itself or for some of its complications (e.g., viral pneumonia, bacterial co-infection, or respiratory failure) is higher than in the general population. We chose influenza for one of the four outcomes of interest because it is characterized by an acute seasonal outbreak, and vaccination and the availability of pharmacies can have an impact on hospital admissions and mortality.

Diabetes

The prevalence of diabetes, a chronic syndrome, is increasing among all ages. Without proper management, over time diabetes can cause cardiovascular, renal, neural, and ocular damage. For this reason, the World Health Organization suggests several preventive strategies, but if a diagnosis is confirmed, it is essential to obtain a tight control of blood sugar through diet and pharmacological approaches. The number and the density of pharmacies can influence both blood sugar level testing and adherence to therapy.

Coronary Syndromes

The coronary syndromes are chronic diseases with multiple possible acute recurrences. The definition of *coronary syndrome* is wide and is related to all coronary heart diseases that cause frequent and lethal acute manifestations, such as myocardial infarction and heart failure. Coronary diseases have a different development than diabetes. Their first manifestation could be more frequently lethal. For this reason, the prevention of these acute events is a cornerstone of the management suggested by the World Health Organization. It is based on diet, physical activity, smoking cessation, and blood pressure control. The first three preventive actions are the goal of global public health strategies, based on awareness campaigns, but community pharmacies could contribute to the prevention and effective treatment of hypertension. Pharmacies play a role in facilitating both adherence to treatment and blood pressure monitoring. They also distribute lipid-lowering medications, for which adherence is a well-known problem.

Upper Gastrointestinal Bleeding

Nonsteroidal anti-inflammatory drugs, the most widely used pain-killers, may increase the risk of upper gastrointestinal bleeding in absence of a correct preventive strategy. Access to pharmacies may affect overuse of nonsteroidal anti-inflammatory drugs, thus increasing the risk of upper gastrointestinal bleeding. On the other hand, it can also help increase adherence to therapy with proton pump inhibitors, as well as with some H2 antagonists, which treat, among other ailments, stomach ulcers and acid reflux. These drugs are some of the most used worldwide, with a long-term indication, and may prevent bleeding due to the long-term use of painkillers.

DATA SOURCES

For the analysis based on the municipality-level data (described below), we obtained the total number of admissions/hospital discharge records aggregated by sex, age class, municipality, and calendar year for selected causes of hospital admission over the period 2000–2015. Hospital discharge records contain details about the main and secondary discharge diagnoses, the implemented operations, and clinical discharge information.[5] For the analysis based on province-level data (also described below), we obtained data from the Health for All database (HFA).[6] The HFA database, maintained by the World Health Organization, brings together selected indicators on demographics, health status, health determinants, and risk factors at the national or subnational level.[7] To obtain province-specific measures of mortality and admission rates, we averaged the yearly rates for five years (2010–2014 for mortality and 2011–2015 for admissions).[8]

This section illustrates the results of two different approaches to estimating the impact of the availability of pharmacies on health outcomes. The first uses cross-sectional data on Italian provinces to examine the demographic rule that links the number of pharmacies to the population size in each city. This variability in pharmacies per capita across provinces can be used to estimate the effect of interest. The second approach uses city-level data and the specific nature of the demographic rule, which provides for sharp steps, as illustrated in Figure 4.1.

The Number of Pharmacies in Italian Municipalities

Our data set includes the number, exact location, date of first opening, and changes of ownership of pharmacies in each municipality (the Italian government collects the data for administrative reasons).[9] The data set includes observations for 7,948 municipalities.[10] As a result of the demographic rule, the number of pharmacies is linked, although imperfectly, with the local population. This is shown clearly in Figure 4.2, which reports the number of pharmacies in each Italian municipality and the local population in 2015. Still, there are deviations from the demographic rule, which are particularly frequent in small municipalities (with less than 12,500 inhabitants). For these towns and villages in rural areas, the constraint imposed by the demographic rule is not binding, and the number of pharmacies is systematically higher than the values predicted by the demographic rule. However, in larger cities, it is not uncommon to observe fewer pharmacies than the predicted number.

Table 4.1 provides summary statistics. On average, municipalities have just 2.2 pharmacies, reflecting the small size of most Italian municipalities. Only 5 percent of municipalities have 6 or more pharmacies. About 14 percent have no pharmacies. The number of inhabitants per pharmacy varies across municipalities. The average is 2,808, but there is significant variability. About 50 percent of municipalities have fewer

Table 4.1 Summary Statistics on the Number of Pharmacies in Italian Municipalities

Variable	N	Mean	S.d.	p5	p10	p25	p50	p75	p90	p95
Number of pharmacies	7,948	2.22	11.78	0	0	1	1	2	4	6
Inhabitants/ number of pharmacies	6,834	2,808	1,697	569	784	1,383	2,585	3,995	5,032	5,845

NOTE: The table reports the number of observations, the mean, standard deviation (S.d.), and percentiles (5th, 10th, 25th, 50th, 75th, 90th, and 95th) of the distribution of each variable (2015).
SOURCE: Authors' calculations based on data from Istat and Italian Ministry of Health.

than 2,585 inhabitants for each pharmacy. About 25 percent have more than 4,000. This illustrates the effects of the delays in implementing the 2012 reform, which set a target of 3,300 inhabitants for each pharmacy.

Results from Data at the Province Level

When using the 2010 population as the denominator, the mean observed density of pharmacies by province was 3.04 per 10,000 inhabitants, with a range of 2.16 and 6.30 per 10,000 inhabitants, while the mean expected density of pharmacies was 2.85 per 10,000 inhabitants with a range between 2.28 and 6.53 per 10,000 inhabitants. Thus, both densities varied widely over provinces.[11] Both the observed and the expected densities depend on the distribution of the population size of the municipalities within each province. This is depicted in Figure 4.3, in which observed and expected densities are plotted against the province-specific median population size of municipalities. The median population size explained 31 percent of the variation in expected pharmacies and 27 percent of the variation in observed pharmacies.

The age-standardized admission rates per 10,000 inhabitants for the period 2011–2015 was between 28.5 and 144.4 for influenza/pneumonia, 45.1 and 120.4 for AMI, and 5.3 and 60.5 for diabetes. Figure 4.4 shows maps with province- and gender-specific age-standardized admission rates for the three outcomes of interest.

While for influenza/pneumonia there was a clear north-south gradient, the rates for the other two outcomes did not follow straightforward geographical patterns. Table 4.2 summarizes the results of the regres-

**Figure 4.3 Province-Specific Observed and Expected Densities of
Pharmacies by Median Municipality Population**

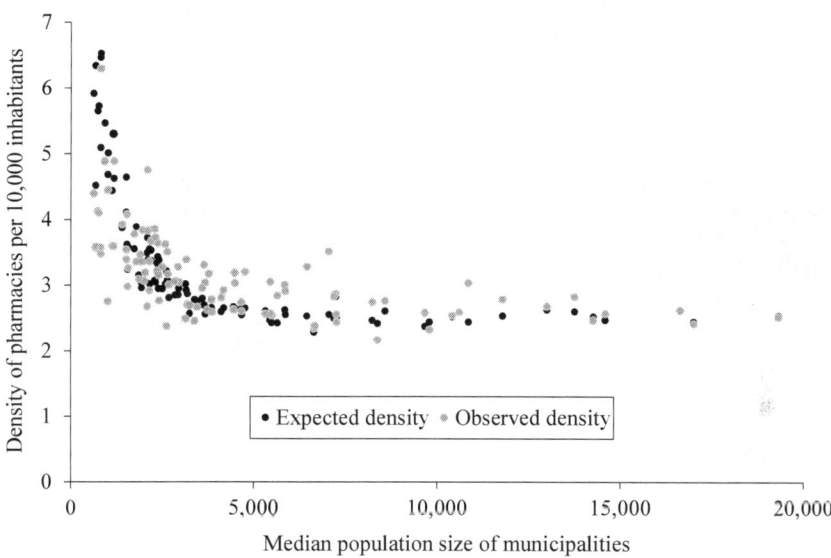

SOURCE: Authors' calculations based on data from Istat and Italian Ministry of Health.

sion models carried out to estimate the association between observed/
expected densities of pharmacies and age-standardized admission or
mortality rates of influenza/pneumonia, AMI, and diabetes.[12] Estimates
reported in the table should be interpreted as the estimated increase or
decrease in admission or mortality rates by a unit increase in expected
or observed province density of pharmacies (i.e., an increase in 1 pharmacy per 10,000 inhabitants). For example, the coefficient of −8.7 in the
upper left corner of the table implies an estimated decrease of 8.7 per
10,000 in the age-standardized rate of influenza/pneumonia admissions
associated with an increase of 1 per 10,000 inhabitants in the observed
number of pharmacies.

The adjusted estimates account for other determinants of the three
outcomes of interest, namely urbanization level, macro geographical
area (North, Central, and South Italy) and educational level. For both
the observed and the expected density of pharmacies, we also conducted
a sensitivity analysis, restricting the sample to provinces with less than

**Figure 4.4 Gender-Specific and Age-Standardized Admission Rates
(per 10,000 inhabitants) for Influenza/Pneumonia, Acute
Myocardial Infarction (AMI) and Diabetes, by Italian
Provinces, 2013**

Influenza/Pneumonia, Males, 65+
Mean: 87.5 per 10,000 inhabitants

Influenza/Pneumonia, Females, 65+
Mean: 45.5 per 10,000 inhabitants

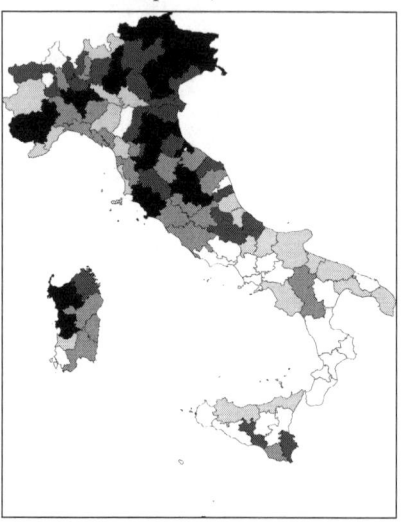

AMI, Males, 65+
Mean: 80.8 per 10,000 inhabitants

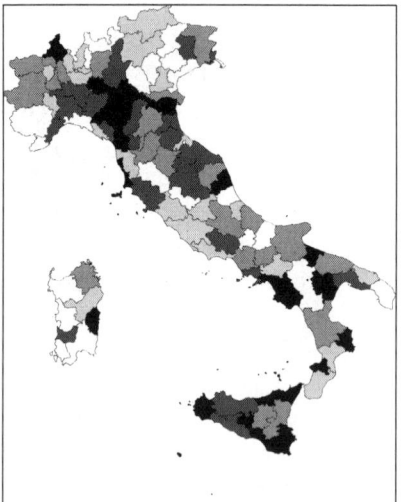

AMI, Females, 65+
Mean: 39.5 per 10,000 inhabitants

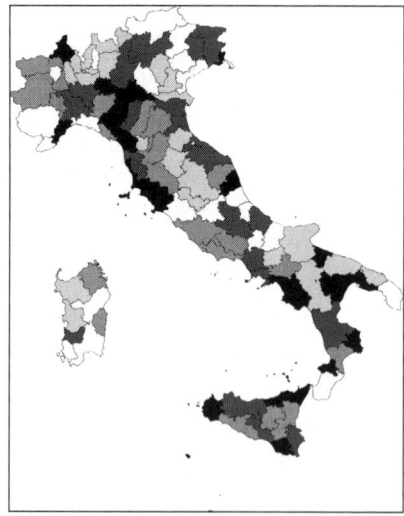

Figure 4.4 (continued)

Diabetes, Males, 45+
Mean: 17.1 per 10,000 inhabitants

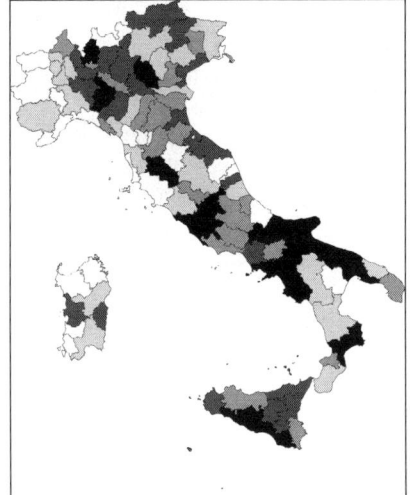

Diabetes, Females, 45+
Mean: 10.2 per 10,000 inhabitants

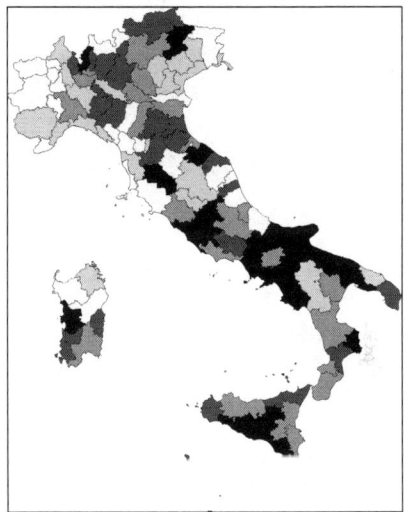

NOTE: Shades indicate quintiles, where the darkest shade corresponds to the highest rate.
SOURCE: Health for All database.

1,000,000 inhabitants. This analysis aimed at checking that our results were not biased by the contribution of large cities in which the access to pharmacies and their density may be different compared to the rest of the country.

It should be noted that geographical patterns associated with both the density of pharmacies and the rates of hospitalization or death could hide or emphasize the estimated associations. Overall, we find no evidence of association between the observed or expected density of pharmacies and admission rates for AMI and diabetes. There is an inverse association between the observed density of pharmacies and admission rates of influenza/pneumonia, although this association was strongly attenuated in the analysis on the expected density of pharmacy. We find no evidence of association with mortality for influenza/pneumonia, AMI, or diabetes for the observed or for the expected density of pharmacies. Results from the analyses restricted to provinces with a popula-

Table 4.2 Association of Observed and Expected Densities of Pharmacies with Admission and Mortality Rates of Influenza/Pneumonia, Acute Myocardial Infarction and Diabetes

Density of pharmacies	Influenza/pneumonia		Acute myocardial infarction		Diabetes	
	Admission rates	Mortality rates	Admission rates	Mortality rates	Admission rates	Mortality rates
Observed density of pharmacies						
Crude	−8.66***	−0.68*	−0.52	1.24	−0.12	0.14
	(2.96)	(0.38)	(1.95)	(0.98)	(0.99)	(0.77)
R^2	0.069	0.031	0.001	0.016	< 0.001	< 0.001
Adjusted coefficient[a]	−8.47***	−0.33	−0.20	1.06	−0.45	−0.33
	(2.53)	(0.24)	(2.08)	(1.01)	(0.99)	(0.39)
R^2	0.443	0.669	0.057	0.138	0.165	0.787
Adjusted and restricted coefficient[a]	−8.52***	−0.29	−0.38	1.11	−0.16	−0.23
	(2.62)	(0.26)	(2.25)	(0.93)	(1.01)	(0.40)
R^2	0.440	0.643	0.052	0.148	0.148	0.764
Expected density of pharmacies[b]						
Crude	0.72	0.42*	−1.92	−0.84	−0.62	−1.08
	(2.02)	(0.25)	(1.26)	(0.64)	(0.65)	(0.49)
R^2	0.001	0.028	0.002	0.017	0.009	0.046
Adjusted coefficient[a]	−2.89	0.02	−1.63	−0.15	−0.31	−0.24
	(1.76)	(0.16)	(1.38)	(0.68)	(0.67)	(0.26)
R^2	0.395	0.663	0.070	0.129	0.165	0.787
Adjusted and restricted coefficient[a]	−2.72	0.02	−1.73	−0.24	−0.33	−0.29
	(1.80)	(0.17)	(1.47)	(0.62)	(−0.66)	(0.26)
R^2	0.388	0.638	0.070	0.136	0.150	0.766

[a] Adjusted for proportion of population living in areas with low urbanization, macro geographical area, proportion of the population with high educational level; restricted to provinces with less than 1,000,000 inhabitants.

[b] Based on the 1991 legislation.

NOTE: *significant at the 0.10 level; **significant at the 0.05 level; ***significant at the 0.01 level. Based on 102 provinces; 92 provinces in the restricted analyses.

SOURCE: Authors' calculations based on data from Istat, Health for All, and Italian Ministry of Health.

tion size lower than 1,000,000 are consistent with the results carried out on all provinces, with no evidence of bias introduced by large cities.

Results from Data at Municipality Level

Data at the municipality level were used to exploit the arbitrary values taken by a specific step of the demographic rule described in Figure 4.1. We focus on one specific step in the demographic rule (at 7,500 inhabitants) for the 2005–2011 period. This choice is motivated by the fact that the step has not changed since the introduction of this type of regulation in the 1960s, which allows us to explore the long-run effects of the regulation. Moreover, most Italian municipalities are small, which implies that there are many observations around the threshold. We select 1,214 municipalities with populations between 5,000 and 10,000, creating a symmetric window (±2,500) around the step and merge data on the number and location of each pharmacy in each municipality with data from hospital discharges.[13] This is a relatively homogeneous sample of small towns and villages. On average, municipalities in this sample have 1.7 pharmacies. Hence, the opening of one pharmacy can potentially make a difference for consumers.

Table 4.3 reports the average number of admissions and the average number of pharmacies in the sample. Figure 4.5 reports the average

Table 4.3 Summary Statistics for Number of Yearly Admissions for the Selected Health Outcomes and Number of Pharmacies

Variable	Mean	S.d.	Min	Max
Upper gastrointestinal bleeding	3.52	2.46	0	26
Coronary diseases	21.28	10.02	0	80
Diabetes	0.49	1.16	0	45
Influenza	15.29	9.43	0	77
Number of pharmacies	1.78	0.67	0	5
Number of pharmacies according to the demographic rule	1.35	0.47	1	2
Observations		8,498		

NOTE: Each observation corresponds to one city in one municipality in one year in the 2005–2011 period.

SOURCE: Authors' calculations based on data from Istat, Health for All, and Italian Ministry of Health.

Figure 4.5 Average Number of Pharmacies and Population

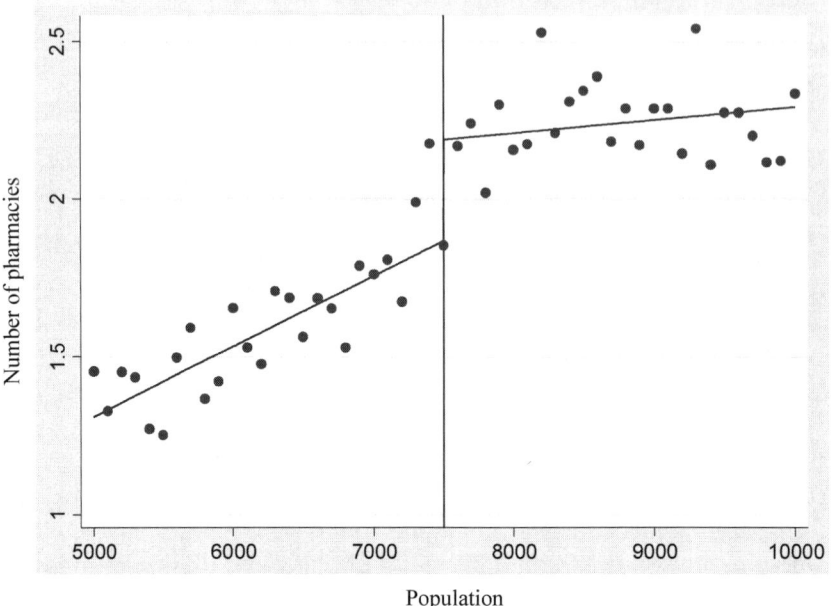

Population

NOTE: The figure reports the average number of pharmacies in municipalities of different size according to historical population (intervals of 100 inhabitants). The lines
are the fitted values of a linear regression of number of pharmacies on population on
each sides of the 7,500 threshold, which corresponds to an increase from one to two
pharmacies according to the demographic rule in place until 2011.
SOURCE: Authors' calculations based on data from Istat, Health for All, and Italian
Ministry of Health.

number of pharmacies for municipalities of different size. Each dot in
the figure corresponds to the average number of pharmacies in a specific interval of 100 between 5,000 and 10,000 inhabitants. The lines on
both sides of the vertical line are the fitted values of a linear regression
on each side of the 7,500 threshold (vertical line), which corresponds to
an increase from one to two pharmacies according to the demographic
rule. The discontinuity at the threshold corresponds to a 0.28 increase
in the number of pharmacies.[14] This is in line with the fact that regulation induces an increase in the number of pharmacies at the threshold,
although other variables may also influence the observed number of
pharmacies.

Figure 4.6 Average Number of Influenza Admissions and Population

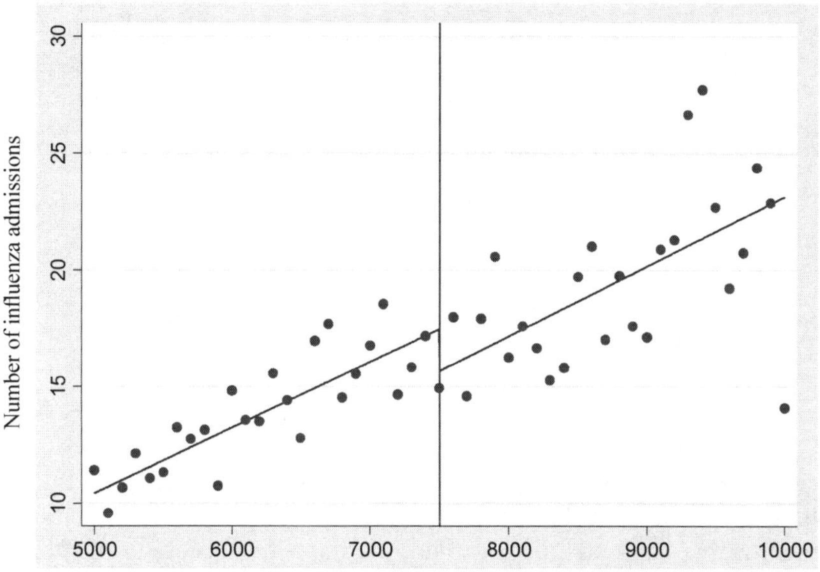

NOTE: The figure reports the average number of influenza admissions in municipalities of different size according to historical population (intervals of 100 inhabitants). The lines are the fitted values of a linear regression of number of admissions on population on each sides of the 7,500 thresholds, which corresponds to an increase from one to two pharmacies according to the demographic rule in place until 2011.

SOURCE: Authors' calculations based on data from Istat, Health for All, and Italian Ministry of Health.

Figure 4.6 shows the corresponding results for the average number of influenza admissions. In this case, there is a negative jump at the threshold of 2.1 cases (statistically significant at 5 percent confidence level). Hence, Figures 4.5 and 4.6 suggest that the increase in the number of pharmacies caused by the threshold is associated with a significant decrease in the number of influenza admissions. The magnitude of the effect is sizable. An increase in the average number of pharmacies of 0.28 (as in Figure 4.5) corresponds to a drop of about 2.1 in the average number of hospital admissions. Hence, a 16 percent increase in the number of pharmacies corresponds to a 13 percent reduction in the average number of influenza related admissions. We find no similar effects for the other health outcomes.

In conclusion, this approach focuses on a subsample of small municipalities in which about half are above and below the threshold. The threshold remained in place for a long time and provides for a relatively large increase in the availability of pharmacies. Hence, the results suggest the existence of a negative long-run effect of the availability of pharmacies on the number of hospital admissions related to influenza.

CONCLUDING REMARKS AND IMPLICATIONS FOR POLICY

This case study examined the impact of regulation on the number and location of pharmacies in Italy and its potential effects on human health. We used health outcomes measures from hospital admission records that can potentially capture the impact of access to medicines (and the other services provided in pharmacies) on the health of the population.

The results from the analysis at the province level support the hypothesis of an inverse association between density of pharmacies and admission rates of influenza. Results using municipality-level data provide complementary and potentially more valid evidence, as they are biased to a lesser extent by geographical confounding. These results are consistent with the results obtained from the analysis of the data at the province level and suggest a long-run effect of pharmacy availability on consumer health. In either analytical approach we find no evidence of association between the density of pharmacies and admission rates for AMI and diabetes or upper gastrointestinal bleeding as a marker of potential negative effects of an increased number of pharmacies.

Overall, the results provide the first evidence on how regulation of the market for pharmacies might affect service availability (a crucial determinant of quality in this market) and consumer health. While these are promising results, they should be interpreted with care. Longer time series could be used in future research to detect the dynamic effects of the availability of pharmacies. Regression discontinuity designs can capture the long-run effects, but they provide results that are difficult to extrapolate out of the sample, as these techniques focus on a very specific sample.

From a policy perspective, our results suggest that restrictions to the number of pharmacies might negatively affect health outcomes of the population. Increasing availability of pharmacies may not only have positive economic effects (e.g., lower prices for unregulated products) but also positive health effects. Guaranteeing a sufficient availability of pharmacies in rural areas may be difficult due to the low profitability of these markets. However, direct subsidies to rural pharmacies seem to be a better policy option than entry restrictions over the entire range of market size. Although strict regulation of the pharmacy market can be justified by the possible dangers associated with the improper use of medicine, it is important to consider the specific effects of entry regulation separately from the regulation of the use and prescription of drugs. We did not find an association between increased competition in the pharmacy market and decreased safety standards, at least in terms of the measured side effects of drugs. To the contrary, the availability of pharmacies and competent pharmacists might have positive effects on health.

Notes

1. Unfortunately, Italy is among the countries not included in the analysis.
2. In 2005, England revised its "control of entry test" system. In 2002, Ireland revoked the rules for the opening of new pharmacies, and in 1998, the Netherlands abolished restrictions on the establishment of new pharmacies. Norway deregulated in 2001, and Sweden, in 2009, ended the monopoly of the state-owned pharmacy company, owner of all pharmacies.
3. The market was subject to a modest liberalization in 2006, when para-pharmacies and supermarkets were allowed to enter the market and sell OTC drugs. The new regulations were introduced by decree-law at the end of June 2006 and converted into law by the Italian parliament at the beginning of August.
4. Attending physicians are not allowed to distribute drugs.
5. The Italian health care system is a regionally based national health service that provides free universal coverage at the point of service. Providers are paid for their activities by means of a prospective payment system based on diagnosis related groups. In order to allocate each patient to a specific diagnosis related group, the Italian Ministry of Health has implemented the hospital discharge records (HDRs) system at a national scale (Ferrè et al. 2014). Hospital discharge records are used to collect information about individual patients such as inpatient data, details of implemented therapies/operations, and clinical discharge information. Hospital

discharge record collection is mandatory, and includes both ordinary and outpatient admissions (day hospital). The records are first collected at the regional level and then forwarded to the Italian Ministry of Health.

6. The HFA database is accessible through the website of the National Institute of Statistics (ISTAT) at the following address: https://www.istat.it/it/archivio/14562 (accessed June 22, 2022).

7. Specifically, the data on hospital admissions is provided by ISTAT based on HDR data. ISTAT is also responsible for the collection and coding of mortality data at the national level.

8. The analysis was limited to a five-year period because the boundaries and number of Italian provinces have changed over time, and a longer period time would have implied a restriction to a smaller number of provinces. In our analysis, we excluded only data for the Sardinia region, which includes a small proportion of the Italian population (less than 3 percent).

9. Italian Ministry of Health, http://www.dati.salute.gov.it (accessed December 13, 2021).

10. We exclude a few municipalities that were created after 2006 or changed name during the same period. We also exclude temporary points of sale (e.g., open only in summer in tourist areas) or smaller branches of authorized pharmacies (e.g., open in tourist areas and/or in specific periods), which are not subject to the demographic rule.

11. The correlation coefficient between observed and expected densities is 0.71.

12. The table reports the estimated regression coefficient of pharmacy density, its standard error, and the regression R^2.

13. In the regression discontinuity analysis, we use the maximum historical population method proposed by Calzolari et al. (2013). In practice, the discontinuity is based on the maximum population in the 1971–2001 period instead of current population to account for the fact that the number of pharmacies does not adjust downward when the population shrinks. See Calzolari et al. (2013) for a detailed discussion of this method.

14. Statistically significant at the 5 percent confidence level.

References

Altowaijri, Abdulaziz, Ceri J. Phillips, and Deborah Fitzsimmons. 2013. "A Systematic Review of the Clinical and Economic Effectiveness of Clinical Pharmacist Intervention in Secondary Prevention of Cardiovascular Disease." *Journal Managed Care Pharmacy* 19(5): 408–416.

Anell, Anders. 2005. "Deregulating the Pharmacy Market: The Case of Iceland and Norway." *Health Policy* 75(1): 9–17.

Blalock, Susan J., Andrew W. Roberts, Julie C. Lauffenburger, Trey Thompson, and Shanna K. O'Connor. 2013. "The Effect of Community Pharmacy–

Based Interventions on Patient Health Outcomes: A Systematic Review." *Medical Care Research and Review* 70(3): 235–266.

Bocci, Michele. 2016. "Il Flop Delle Nuove Farmacie." *La Repubblica*, May 30.

Calzolari, Giacomo, Francesco Manaresi, Andrea Ichino, and Viki Nellas. 2013. "When the Baby Cries at Night: Inelastic Buyers in Non-Competitive Markets." Bank of Italy Working Paper No. 914. Rome: Bank of Italy.

Chisholm-Burns, Marie A., Jeannie Kim Lee, Christina A. Spivey, Marion Slack, Richard N. Herrier, Elizabeth Hall-Lipsy, Joshua Graff Zivin, Ivo Abraham, John Palmer, Jennifer R. Martin, Sandra S. Kramer, and Timothy Wunz. 2010. "US Pharmacists' Effect as Team Members on Patient Care: Systematic Review and Meta-Analyses." *Medical Care* 48(10): 923–933.

Cooper, Richard J. 2013. "Over-the-Counter Medicine Abuse—A Review of the Literature." *Journal of Substance Use* 18(2): 82–107.

Ferré, Francesca, Antonio Giulio de Belvis, Luca Valerio, Silvia Longhi, Agnese Lazzari, Giovanni Fattore, Walter Ricciardi, and Anna Maresso. 2014. "Italy: Health System Review." *Health Systems in Transition* 16(4):1–168.

Gai, Yunwei, and Li Feng. 2017. "Relationship between Pharmacist Density and Adult Influenza Vaccination after Controlling for Individual and Neighborhood Effects." *Journal of the American Pharmacists Association* 57(4): 474–482.

Huang, Wan-Ting, Chih-His Chang, Yu-Fen Hsu, and Jen-Hsiang Chuang. 2015. "Prognostic Factors for Mortality in Patients Hospitalized with Influenza Complications, in Taiwan." *International Health* 7(1): 73–75.

Kirkdale, Charlotte L., Guillaume Nebout, Francis Megerlin, and Tracy Thornley. 2017. "Benefits of Pharmacist-Led Flu Vaccination Services in Community Pharmacy." *Annales Pharmaceutiques Françaises* 75(1): 3–8.

Koshman, Sheri L., Theresa L. Charrois, Scot H. Simpson, Finlay A. McAlister, and Ross T. Tsuyuki. 2008. "Pharmacist Care of Patients with Heart Failure: A Systematic Review of Randomized Trials." *Archives of Internal Medicine* 168(7): 687–694.

Mocetti, Sauro. 2016 "Dynasties in Professions and the Role of Rents and Regulation: Evidence from Italian Pharmacies." *Journal of Public Economics* 133: 1–10.

Nazar, Hamde, Zacharia Nazar, Jane Portlock, Adam Todd, and Sarah P. Slight. 2015. "A Systematic Review of the Role of Community Pharmacies in Improving the Transition from Secondary to Primary Care." *British Journal of Clinical Pharmacology* 80(5): 936–948.

Pagliero, Mario. 2015. *The Effects of Recent Reforms Liberalizing Regulated Professions in Italy*. Report for the European Commission. Brussels: European Commission.

Pousinho, Sarah, Manuel Morgado, Amílcar Falcão, and Gilberto Alves. 2016. "Pharmacist Interventions in the Management of Type 2 Diabetes Mellitus: A Systematic Review of Randomized Controlled Trials." *Journal of Managed Care & Specialty Pharmacy* 22(5): 493–515.

Schaumans, Catherine, and Frank Verboven. 2008. "Entry and Regulation: Evidence from Health Care Professions." *Rand Journal of Economics* 39(4): 949–972.

Tsuyuki, Ross T., Yazid N. Al Hamarneh, Charlotte A. Jones, and Brenda R. Hemmelgarn. 2016. "The Effectiveness of Pharmacist Interventions on Cardiovascular Risk: The Multicenter Randomized Controlled RxEACH Trial." *Journal of the American College of Cardiology* 67(24): 2846–28454.

Vogler, Sabine, Katharina Habimana, and Danielle Arts. 2014. "Does Deregulation in Community Pharmacy Impact Accessibility of Medicines, Quality of Pharmacy Services and Costs? Evidence from Nine European Countries." *Health Policy* 117(3): 311–327.

5
Deregulation of the Legal Professions in Poland

A Trade-off between Market Growth and Professionalism?

Piotr Białowolski
*Kozminski University and
Harvard T.H. Chan School of Public Health*

Michał Masior
Lazarski University

INSTITUTIONAL CONTEXT

In 2004 and 2005, Poland deregulated access to the legal professions. This provides an interesting case study of the effect of reforms that aim to lower the barriers to entry to the legal market. Professional conduct and adequate qualification are often the product of institutional incentives. Regulation of legal services, such as representation before court or a counsel, hinges on lawyers as service providers and their group representation, such as bar associations. Lowering barriers to entry to the profession naturally raises questions about whether that affects the quality of legal service; therefore, a key question we seek to answer is whether such reforms negatively affected service quality.

Public interest in the regulation of legal services rests on the idea that the work of legal professionals is inexorably linked to the effectiveness of the administration of justice, administrative procedures, quality of law, social ties, and general trust toward the state and the law (Boon 2014). Smooth functioning of the market for legal services can be hampered by the asymmetry of information, negative externalities, and the collective action problem (Decker and Yarrow 2010). State regulation has traditionally counterbalanced the promotion of the collective interests of lawyers as put forth by their bar associations.

REGULATORY CONTEXT

The regulatory regime for any occupational group consists of rules that define entry to the profession and are complemented by rules of conduct, both of which have an economic impact. For instance, the scope of exclusive rights or legal protection of a professional title determines the value of economic rents the practitioners can extract.

In Poland, legal trainees are required to obtain a law degree, which takes five years to complete. Because most trainees graduate from public universities, the cost of their higher education is covered by the state. Subsequently, they decide whether they want to pursue a career as a qualified lawyer. If they decide to follow such a path, they are required to enroll in a bar training course organized by one of the two major legal professions in the country: advocates (*adwokaci*) or legal advisors (*radcowie prawni*) (both professions suggest that their professional titles are translated into English as *attorney-at-law*). Until 2009, bar training took three and a half years; after the reform, it was three years. Upon completion of the bar training, candidates are expected to take the bar exam, which, upon passing, entitles them to the professional title of an advocate or a legal advisor. Following the completion of the mandatory education, training, and examinations, freshman lawyers must purchase membership to the bar association and civil liability insurance, and they have to participate in continuous professional development. Since 2004, when the legal professions lost monopoly on legal services, the law graduates can also become so-called legal counselors (*doradcy prawni*), that is, lawyers who render legal services without formal bar training or having passed the bar exam.

Before 2004, only advocates were eligible to provide all types of legal services (including legal counsel), and any violations might have resulted in criminal charges. Legal advisors were not allowed to assume any family, custody, and delinquency cases. These and other similar market constraints were partially lifted during the economic and political transition in Poland in the 1990s and early 2000s. Exclusive rights of advocates and legal advisors to provide legal counsel were abolished, while exclusive rights of advocates to provide representation in court were significantly reduced. As a result, starting in 2004 all members of the general public are allowed to provide some forms of legal counsel, such as draft legal documents, give legal advice, or represent a party in front of a first-instance civil court. This change attracted new entrants, mostly legal counselors, who are lawyers without a professional title.

Other amendments soon followed suit. After the transition to a market economy, legal education in the 1990s started to attract many students. However, despite completing a law degree, restrictions on the number of bar trainee positions, nepotism, and difficulty in attending examinations in various local bar locations prevented many graduates from becoming qualified lawyers. To illustrate this, between 1999 and 2003, each year the number of law graduates exceeded 7,000, whereas the number of accepted trainees to advocate and legal advisor bar remained below 1,000. Consequently, a vast majority of law graduates became disconnected from their profession. This situation created political pressure for a change. The conditions became favorable when in 2004 the Polish Constitutional Tribunal pronounced a judgment requesting a change in the rules of entry to the profession (prerequisites and selection criteria), and the provisions limiting the number of trainees were deemed unconstitutional. In response, a new law in 2005 required the Ministry of Justice and the bar associations to jointly organize standardized annual exams to the bar training and to guarantee access to the profession for all applicants scoring above a predefined passing threshold. Starting in 2010, trainees had to take a state exam to verify that they acquired sufficient knowledge and skills to deal with most common legal tasks, such as preparing an appeal to a court ruling or drafting a contract or a legal opinion. Minor amendments to these so-called advocate and legal advisor exams were introduced in 2013.

Another development was the delineation of new paths to legal professions. These paths allowed for circumventing bar training for those lawyers who were able to gain enough professional experience without bar training. Additionally, PhD degree holders in law and some other groups of legal professionals such as judges or prosecutors, who had sufficient, four-year legal experience, became eligible to enlist as advocates or legal advisors without the requirement to pass the final exam. These new paths to the profession deprived the bar associations of full control over the process of admission.

All amendments that came along with new regulations raised doubts about the level of professionalism of advocates and legal advisors admitted under the new rules. Additionally, questions were raised regarding unfair competition between qualified and nonqualified legal service practitioners. Licensing was practically abolished for most of the legal services in the market, and it was not substituted by certification or registration. The monolith group of lawyers rendering their services to the market began to be composed of at least four subgroups: 1) older advocates and legal advisors who made it to the profession before the reforms; 2) a younger generation of lawyers who underwent the bar training having passed the state exams instead of bar exams; 3) advocates and legal advisors who did not attend a bar training at all, working previously as, for instance, prosecutors or legal academics; and 4) practitioners who entered the market but not the profession (usually holding just a law degree). In practice, the fourth subgroup turned out to be relatively small and entered only some profitable segments of the market such as debt collection or injury compensation. The academics and other legal professionals who gained the right to provide legal services entered in modest numbers. Overall, the reform raised the question of whether a constantly growing number of new practitioners (group 2) acts more professionally than the group of lawyers who gained their credentials before the reform (group 1). Evidence from Japan shows that the liberalization of rules of entry to the profession led to a deterioration in the quality of legal services and subsequent loss of public trust in lawyers, but the effect was shown to come from the conduct of the elder members of the profession and the new entrants (Ishida 2017; Ota 2014). To this end, this chapter investigates the effects of the reforms on various service quality indicators and analyzes the functioning of the market for legal services at the onset of reforms.

IMPACT OF REFORMS ON PRACTITIONERS IN THE MARKET

Prior to the reforms, only advocates had full rights to representation before the courts. After the reforms, those rights were gradually shared with legal advisors, and the entry of external lawyers (with their credentials not verified by bars) became easier. The main focus of the reforms, however, was the bar training. They abolished quotas and introduced nationally standardized examinations, the same for both professions, which aimed at guaranteeing that fulfilment of objective criteria was sufficient to enter the profession. As shown in Tables 5.1–5.3, these changes alone caused a significant inflow of trainees to professional training and subsequently translated into a higher number of advocates and legal advisors. More candidates passed a predefined, standardized threshold on the exam and were accepted to the respective bars, as either advocates or legal advisor trainees.

Overall, the average pass rates increased when the state took over the supervision over the entrance exams (Table 5.1). The number of candidates increased, as did the number of law graduates entering the bar training.

Table 5.1 Pass Rates and the Number of Successful Candidates before and after the Introduction of the New Entrance Examinations to the Bar Training in 2005

	2000–2004	2005–2017
Average pass rate (%), entrance exam for advocate training	31.6	49.1
Average pass rate (%), entrance exam for legal advisor training	26.9	41.3
Average number of candidates who passed the examinations for advocate trainee	293	1,583
Average number of candidates who passed the examinations for legal advisor trainee	760	2,307

SOURCE: Polish Ministry of Justice.

Data from the Polish Ministry of Justice show the number of candidates for an advocate trainee or a legal advisor trainee who passed their entrance exams under the new regulations in December 2005 (1,822 out of 4,526—40 percent on average). These candidates began their training in 2006 and subsequently sat new professional examinations in mid-2010. A total of 1,423 out of 2,086 (68 percent) passed these exams and enlisted as advocates or legal advisors by the end of 2010. Other cohorts followed. Thus, after 2011 the full effects of the 2005 reform could have been observed.

Table 5.2 Number of Lawyers Who Passed the Professional Examinations with or without Prior Bar Training in 2009–2015

Number of candidates taking:	With prior bar training	Without prior bar training	Total
Advocate examination	6,953	354	7,307
Legal advisor examination	12,383	925	13,308
Total	19,336	1,279	20,615

NOTE: In December 2009 only lawyers without prior bar training could seat professional examinations.
SOURCE: Polish Ministry of Justice.

Average pass rates for both the advocate and legal advisor exams stood at 71 percent (data for 2009–2017). Multiplied by the pass rates for the new entrance exams to the bar training, they provide approximate chances for a law graduate to become (four years later) an advocate or legal advisor: 35 percent for the candidates for advocates and 29 percent for the candidates for legal advisors.[1]

Furthermore, as a result of the reform, some candidates were exempted from the bar training and some from the professional examinations. The exemption from the bar training opened a path to both professions for 1,279 nontrainees who passed the professional examinations (from the first professional examinations in 2009 to 2015). They account for 6 percent of the total number of lawyers who passed the professional examinations.

An even larger number of lawyers (4,559) benefited from the second exemption, namely being exempted from both the bar training and the professional examinations. They account for 15 percent of the total registered advocates and legal advisors between 2009 and 2015 (Table 5.3).

Table 5.3 Number of Entries into the Registries of Advocates and Legal Advisors with and without a Prior Professional Examination in 2007–2015

Number of entries into the registry of:	With prior professional exam	Without prior professional exam	Total
Advocates	8,623	2,208	10,831
Legal advisors	16,538	2,351	18,889
Total	25,161	4,559	29,720

SOURCE: Polish Ministry of Justice.

In 2020, lawyers who obtained their professional title according to the amended, more transparent rules constituted around half of the total number of advocates and legal advisors in Poland (35,200 out of around 70,000). The total number of legal professionals (advocates and legal advisors) rose by 140 percent between 2005 and 2020. The number of practicing advocates increased from 6,191 to around 20,400, and that of legal advisors rose from 17,501 to 35,200. At the same time the number of advocates and legal advisors who had the professional title but did not practice increased substantially—from 6,600 by the end of 2004 to around 12,000 by the end of 2017. It is a heterogeneous group, comprised mostly of retired legal professionals, advocates who choose inactivity (such as parents on maternity/paternity leave; advocates cannot provide their services under an employment contract), or those who are not satisfied with their income and decide to follow a different professional path.

To this number one should add at least 5,000 unqualified lawyers (legal counselors) who opened up their businesses since 2004, when the monopoly of advocates and legal advisors in legal services was relaxed. Additionally, it should include an unspecified number of law graduates and other employees who managed to find a job in newly forming law firms. Widening the supply of legal services (measured by the number of practitioners) threefold—from 23,000 in 2004 to at least 60,000 in 2020—within the 15-year period is a significant achievement of the reforms. Its main social value lies in ensuring broader access to law for the society. More transparent exams as well as the exemptions stimulated higher interest in legal professions. Regulatory reforms allowed for a more efficient use of qualified labor.

DIMENSIONS AND MEASUREMENT OF QUALITY IN LEGAL SERVICES

Services in general, and legal services in particular, have three defining attributes: they are relatively intangible, they tend to be produced and consumed simultaneously, and they tend to involve the consumer in the production process (Stewart, Hope, and Muhlemann 2000). Service quality is multidimensional. These dimensions, according to Parasuraman et al. (1988), are reliability, responsiveness, assurance, and empathy. The same applies to legal services. Empirical studies show importance of professional skills, marketing skills, reputation, and ethics for the success of legal professionals (Bialowolski and Weziak-Bialowolska 2021). Good quality legal service encompasses, among other things, availability of a lawyer (e.g., having offices open at hours convenient to clients or communicating with the customer on the telephone, email, and SMS), using clear and understandable language in the communication with a client, and setting out and adhering to clear pricing rules. Professional legal service is correlated with a greater likelihood of recovering disputed amounts of money and increasing the amount recovered (Ross 1980), a higher probability of winning a case in a trial (Hirshleifer and Osborne 2001), and better ability to collect information that matters, especially in common law jurisdictions where courts have less inquisitorial power than in civil law systems (Dewatripont and Tirole 1999).

Quality of legal services is inherently linked to the professionalism of the legal service providers (Boon 2010). This is demonstrated by the mere size of the codes of ethics in the *Model Rules of Professional Conduct* published by the American Bar Association (2018), which is hundreds of pages. Professional codes of conduct and deontology specify the principles and sometimes precise rules lawyers are required to follow. Qualified lawyers and members of the bar are expected to be competent, conscientious, diligent, honest, and prompt, and to respect rules of confidentiality or to act in an efficient manner. The codes govern four types of relations of a lawyer: with a client, with court and offices, with other lawyers, and with the bar or law society authorities (Boon 2014).

Lawyers usually tend to imply that "high quality" is an absolute that requires a service provider to be professionally qualified (Mayson 2016). However, high-quality service usually entails higher price, which excludes lower-income groups from consumption and lowers the value of service for the customers. A more comprehensive and commonly used approach consists then in defining quality in services as the "perceived service quality" by consumers, conceptualized as the gap between customer expectations and their evaluations of the performance of a particular service provider (Brady and Cronin 2001; Buttle 1996; Parasuraman, Zeithaml, and Berry 1985, 1988).

Consequently, measuring the quality of legal services may be conducted with the use of various instruments, including the opinions of customers, opinions of the peers and judges, indicators of substitution effects (e.g., replacing legal service with self-help), or indicators of the objective effects of the legal work (outcome). Other measurement tools include civil liability insurance premia (supposedly lower with high-quality legal services), results of negligence suits against lawyers and peer inspections in law firms (the bar verifies compliance of legal practices with some pre-defined standards), opinions of recruitment specialists (capable of identifying patterns in training and experience), or comparison of the technical requirements for lawyer candidates they have to face during bar exams (Masior 2017).

In this chapter, we use the following measures of quality: opinions of customers as expressed in the complaints they file, and opinions of the peers under the form of the procedural decisions they take in the administration of disciplinary matters in the bar associations. We find these measures to be particularly suitable for capturing low-quality legal services as complaints are filed, and the disciplinary proceedings are usually initiated as a reaction to perceived low-quality service.[2] Thus, we aim to take into account both the perspective of consumers, who usually focus on the soft skills of a lawyer—the facet of service easy for them to perceive—and technical knowledgeability of lawyers and their overall professionalism, as assessed by their peers, who usually check whether they adhered to law and to the rules of professional conduct.

DATA AND METHODS

Following the approach proposed by Ishida (2017), we investigate the number of reported complaints and disciplinary cases. To this end, we use the data gathered by the Polish Bar Council and the National Chamber of Legal Advisors, supreme bodies of the Polish bar associations. The Polish Bar Council has been providing summary reports since 1992 containing the relevant quality measures assessed over three-year periods corresponding to the term in office of advocates' representatives.[3] Because of the lack of earlier data, the analysis was limited to 2010–2016.

Authorized and obliged by law, self-governing bodies (such as the bar associations) control professional conduct of their members (advocates, legal advisors, and trainees); examine complaints filed against their members; and, if necessary, hold them accountable for any violation of the rules of conduct. Rules of ethics are specified in the resolutions of the respective authorities of the bar associations. Codes of ethics regulate legal practice and relations with clients, courts, colleagues, and legal authorities. As such, we proxy the quality of legal services using the frequency and structure of wrongdoings committed by legal professionals. The data include reported breaches of rules of conduct as defined by the lawyers themselves.

Both the district bar councils of advocates and the district chambers of legal advisors handle the cases filed against their members. The cases are investigated by district disciplinary prosecutors and their deputies. Disciplinary prosecutors can file charges to a district disciplinary court (specifically, a request to initiate a disciplinary proceeding) against a member of the bar. If a peer advocate, legal advisor, or a trainee is found guilty, she can appeal to the Higher Disciplinary Court. All disciplinary courts are administered solely by lawyers who are members of the respective bar association.

The data on disciplinary cases describe the consecutive steps of the procedure. We interpret them as follows: should the number of cases exhibit a downward or stable trend as the effects of the reforms were unfolding after 2005 and particularly after 2010 (when newly selected advocates and legal advisors started to obtain the professional title), it would support the hypothesis that lowering the entry requirements did not negatively affect the quality of legal services.

Comparing complaint rates is a common method used to assess the quality of professional services under a number of regulatory regimes. The number of complaints depends on the extent to which a given population is litigious (Kleiner 2006) and on the awareness of legal rights to file complaints with the regulatory body. Filing a complaint is usually a first step in initiating a negligence suit against a member of the profession. It is also the only practical mechanism that allows customers to express their dissatisfaction with the service, even if a practitioner did his work diligently in technical legal terms.

In Poland, clients dissatisfied with the service they received have a right to complain to the bar about their legal representative. In the advocates' bar association, the complaints are addressed in the so-called bureaus of complaints, which decide whether there is any sign of a violation of the professional conduct, and if so, pass the pending cases to a disciplinary prosecutor for investigation. In the legal advisors' bar association, a complaint is handled directly by a disciplinary prosecutor who decides whether to initiate a disciplinary investigation.

IMPACT OF THE REGULATIONS ON THE PROFESSIONALISM OF LAWYERS

Advocates

Complaints or notifications of improper professional conduct are filed by both the lawyers' clients and also the courts, public administration, authorities of the bar, the Ministry of Justice, or other members of the bar (often an opposing party in a legal dispute).[4]

The number of complaints filed against practicing advocates (calculated relative to their number) and the number of cases with identified breaches of the rules of professional conduct show that the discontent about the advocates' performance gradually declined between 2004 and 2016 across all sorts of complainants (Figure 5.1). Judges and clerks in the public administration were less likely to complain against advocates, and this trend was also observed among clients. During 2013–2016, the last reporting period, 7,100 complaints were filed to 24 district bar councils, which translates to 0.5 complaints per practicing advocate over the three-year period (or 0.16 per advocate per year). Overall, the complaints are rarely filed against advocates.

Figure 5.2 shows that the frequency of the most common allegation, a breach of professional duties, fell by two-thirds following the reforms that opened the profession to newcomers. Although the distinction between the categories of allegations is decided subjectively by the bar associations and may not be rigorously respected, the professional duties usually describe the procedural obligations, such as meeting deadlines or participating in hearings. They can relate also to the conduct of the legal business, such as office equipment and signboard, records of cases and financial information, cases assigned by courts,

Figure 5.1 Complaints against Advocates Filed in All District Bar Councils of Advocates (per practicing advocate)

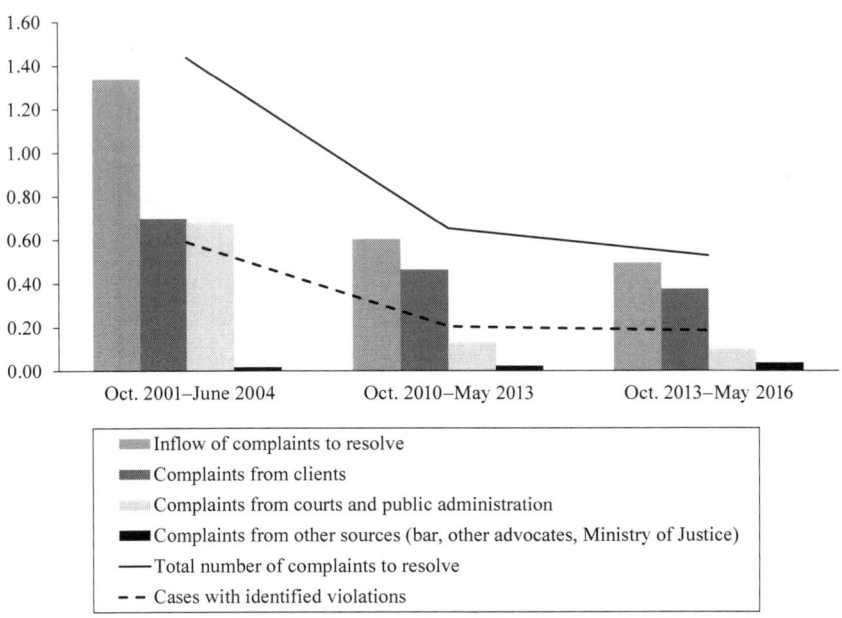

NOTE: The denominator is a three-year average of the number of practicing advocates. The Polish Bar Council reports national data only once in 3 years for the full intervals; data for October 2004–June 2007 and October 2007–June 2010 were not gathered.
SOURCE: Polish Bar Council.

permitted cooperation with other lawyers and professionals, and other related issues. Duties in professional ethics on their part, as mentioned above, describe desired behavior of a lawyer (confidentiality, good manners, honesty, loyalty), and thus can possibly impact clients more directly than breaches in professional duties, which are meant to safeguard clients' interests usually more indirectly. For this reason, fewer allegations related to professional ethics than to professional duties is as positive of a message as the declining rate of breaches in the latter. The frequencies of other types of reported breaches in complaints, including unjust financial settlements with clients (fees) or abuses in the freedom of speech (insults or similar), remained stable at low levels or even slightly declined.

Figure 5.2 Complaints on Advocates by Type of Allegation (per practicing advocate)

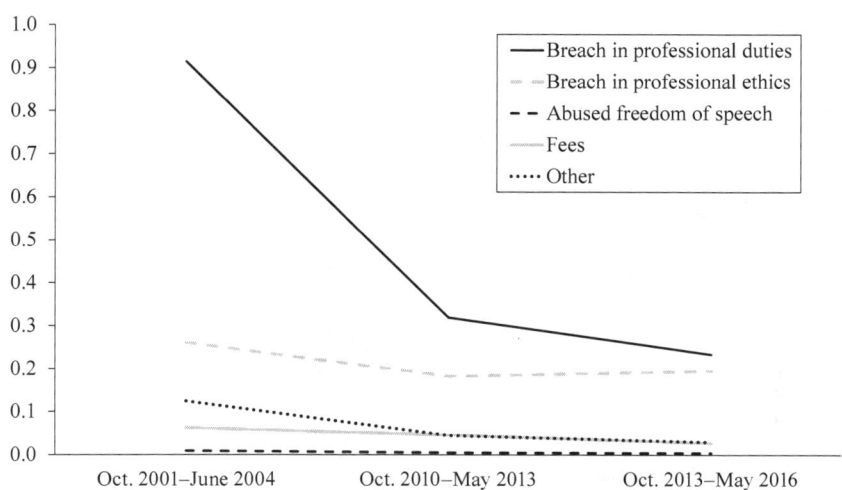

SOURCE: Polish Bar Council.

Despite increased inflow of cases for investigation to the disciplinary prosecutors in the bar councils of advocates between 2004 and 2013, the number of indictments remained relatively stable (Figure 5.1). It may point to relatively little substance in the charges filed.

The relative number of penalties imposed on advocates changed little over the 2001–2016 period (Figure 5.3). Their structure also remained quite similar, although the least severe penalties (warnings and reprimands) were imposed slightly more frequently. The harshest penalty, loss of the right to practice, has been imposed in only about 100 cases. In absolute terms the number of warnings increased from 52 in 2001–2004 to 152 in 2013–2016 (threefold), that of reprimands from 41 to 182 (more than fourfold), and the number of fines from 41 to 121 (threefold). However, given a threefold increase in the number of practicing advocates over that period (from 5,000 in 2001 to 16,000 in 2016), the frequency of penalties per practitioner remained at a very low level (4.2 percent in 2013–2016 for all penalties combined). These statistics are even lower if we consider only legally valid penalties (advocates may challenge the decisions of the first-instance disciplinary courts)—then the frequency of all penalties per practitioner in

Figure 5.3 Penalties Imposed by the First-Instance Disciplinary Courts, Both Legally Valid and Challenged (per practicing advocate)

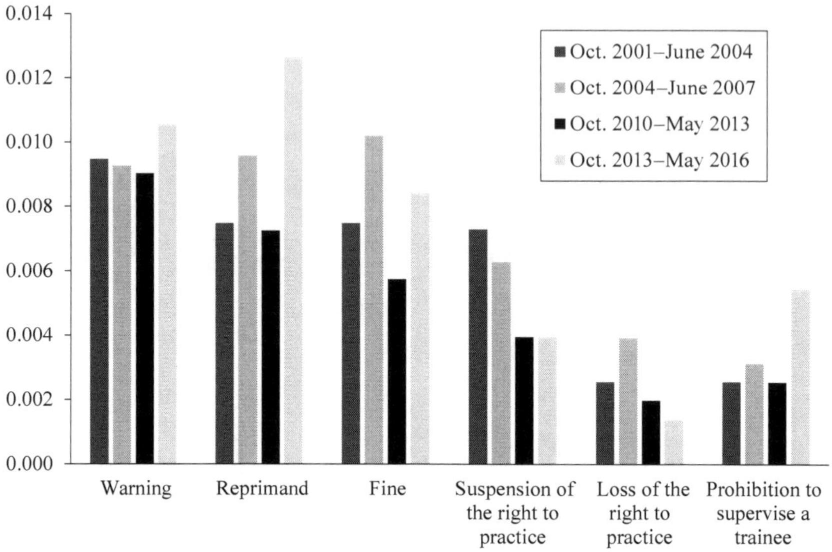

SOURCE: Polish Bar Council.

2013–2016 drops to 2.8 percent (their structure remains similar to that observed for all the penalties).

Notwithstanding their relative minor importance, one can expect that increases in the number of verdicts pointing to breaches in professional ethics—as well as in the number of issued warnings, reprimands, and prohibitions to supervise a trainee—can also be attributable to the more rigorous approach the disciplinary courts have adopted since 2013–2016 as compared to the previous periods.

Legal Advisors

The complaints against legal advisors are resolved by disciplinary prosecutors in the district chambers of legal advisors. Their validity is examined, and the prosecutor assigned to the case decides whether to initiate an investigation, refuse to do so, pass the case to the dean of chamber (in less severe instances) or to a different chamber, try to reach an amicable settlement, or drop the case. Once the prosecutors decide to investigate a case, they can also suspend it or quash an enquiry. Should they find enough evidence against a legal advisor, they file an indictment to a disciplinary court. Similarly, should the dean conclude that a legal advisor committed wrongdoing, he or she can issue a warning. A comparison of the numbers of incoming cases between advocates (0.52 per practicing advocate in the period, mid-2013 to mid-2016) and legal advisors (yearly inflow multiplied by three—0.15 for the three-year period 2014–2016) shows that the frequency of misconduct claims against legal advisors is much lower (Figure 5.4); one reason may be their limited activity in litigation. Despite a short span of the time series, it is noticeable that there has been a decline in the number of cases filed to the chambers between 2010–2013 and 2013–2016 per practicing legal advisor, which may stem from a better conduct of legal advisors.

Figure 5.4 Number of Cases to Investigate by the District Disciplinary Prosecutors (per practicing legal advisor)

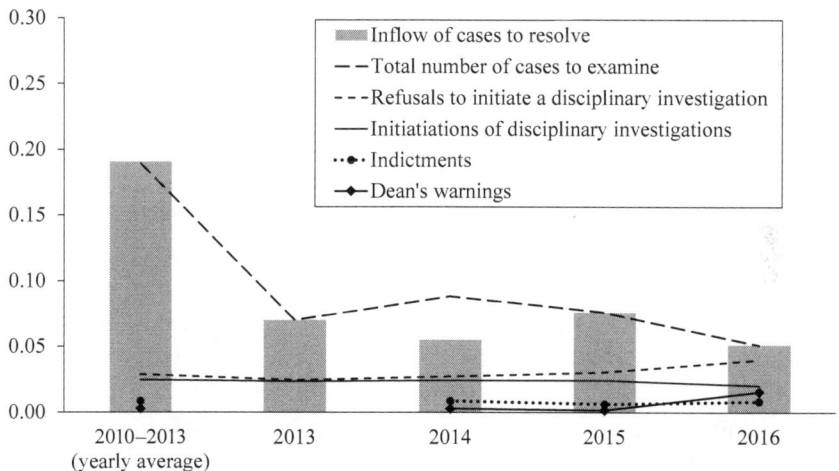

SOURCE: National Chamber of Legal Advisors.

Other indicators of the lack of professionalism, such as indictments and warnings, did not exhibit any significant time trend.[5]

District disciplinary courts of legal advisors received 500–900 cases yearly during the period 2010–2016 (Figure 5.5). The inflow remained steady at the level of 2.2–3.3 percent relative to the population of active

Figure 5.5 Inflow of Cases to District Disciplinary Courts of Legal Advisors (per practicing legal advisor)

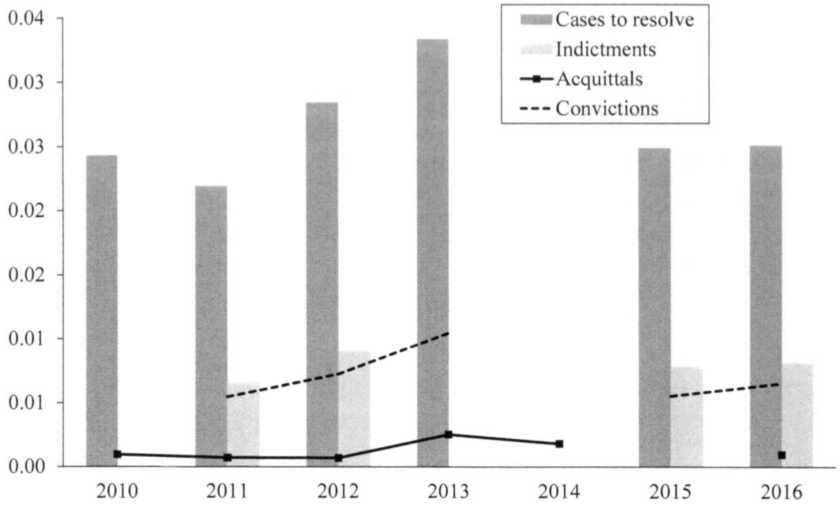

SOURCE: National Chamber of Legal Advisors.

legal advisors. Most of the inflow can be attributed to the appeals from their refusals to file an indictment (1.2–1.6 percent).

Neither the dynamics of cases for investigation by the district disciplinary prosecutors in 2013–2016 nor the dynamics of cases registered in the district disciplinary courts in 2010–2016 exhibit any upward or downward trend. The share of acquittals and convictions in the rulings of the district disciplinary courts between 2010 and 2016 remained relatively stable, suggesting no deterioration in service quality.

The analysis of time series for rulings of the Higher Disciplinary Court of legal advisors in 2005–2016 allows for an identification of a stable upward trend in the number of penalties issued during the period 2005–2010. However, because the effects of the reforms became more apparent around 2011, the number of penalties has been fluctuating since, not exhibiting any particular trend.

Overall, our results show that a rapid increase in the number of legal professionals (that followed the deregulation) did not coincide with an increased number of reported misconducts. A declining number of complaints per practicing advocate, especially those originating from courts, also marks a significant professional improvement that accompanied the reforms. Performance of legal advisors matched that of advocates. Only a very low number of complaints on advocates and legal advisors led to subsequent charges and a conviction by a disciplinary court, a penalty, or a dean's warning.

CONCLUSION AND POLICY IMPLICATIONS

The Polish reforms present an interesting case study on reforming the entry criteria to the legal profession. Several waves of reforms brought about complex changes in the regime of rules of entry that, according to its proponents, aimed to strike the right balance between the private interests of the profession and the common good (public interest). Some of the changes included delicensing the legal counsel, which is the most important part of legal services, while implementing alternative and more transparent sets of requirements for aspiring lawyers. Maintaining a legal protection for their professional titles (*advocate*, *legal advisor*) reduced the need for delicensing some of the legal professions, while easier access to these professions contributed to an expansion in their availability. The data presented in this chapter do not point to a deterioration in the quality of service provided, at least in the sector served by the qualified lawyers. At the same time, they show an increase in the availability of the service as evidenced by the significant growth in the number of practitioners, a clear sign of the value added to the market. Some of this growth can be attributed to the emergence of a group of lawyers with lower levels of education (legal counselors), which would coincide with evidence from the existing literature (Timmons and Thornton 2017, 2019).

The partial deregulation of the market for legal services that occurred in Poland in 2004–2005 changed the institutional setting for legal work, advancing the logic of the market while limiting some of the most alarming examples of self-interested behavior of the bar associations. Leaving most of the rules of conduct unchanged and keeping intact the power of the self-regulatory bar associations helped to maintain the standards of professionalism on the market as defined by the

Polish Bar Council and the National Chamber of Legal Advisors. Also potentially contributing to the outcome are the ties the qualified lawyers, authorized to stand before a court, have with the unregulated law firms that guarantee the retention of the prereform licensing standards for courtroom representation (where the possible negative externalities of the low-quality legal services are likely to be the highest). It is worth mentioning that following the reforms, the bar training improved and the bars professionalized their operations (also because of more anonymous relationships among their members), communicating online and providing more workshops and support for their members, among others. The reforms produced a higher demand for legal education before the exams, which helped to create new preparatory courses, while the officials from the Ministry and the bar associations became more skilled in setting adequate requirements for the exams.

As Mayson (2020) put it, "No regulatory approach can ever be perfect nor can it eradicate all risks to the public" (p. ix). The burden and cost of regulation should be proportionate to the risks involved. It seems that, at least in Poland, there is still some room for improvement. Fair competition may require, for instance, that all practitioners and other providers of legal services are registered and, possibly, also subject to disciplinary liability or ombudsman investigation (Mayson 2020). At the same time, the requirements to obtain the professional title of *advocate* or *legal advisor* and to practice in these professions could be decreased or at least re-evaluated (Devlin 2017; Gordon, Shackel, and Mark 2012; Semple 2013). In Britain, Mayson (2020) finds that competences and ethics of qualified lawyers are not necessarily better than that of the unregulated lawyers. The rules of conduct relating to marketing practices or office premises could be relaxed to allow more space for competition that would help new entrants establish and expand their law firms. Such a reform can be justified on the basis that the junior lawyers are at an inherent disadvantage compared to their older peers as they usually have to build their own client base, and some of the standards imposed by the bar disproportionately constrain their entrepreneurial endeavors. This has become particularly apparent recently in Poland in an increasingly saturated market for legal services.

The Polish case also demonstrates that education, training, and assessment can be used as policy instruments to better meet consumers' needs (Boud and Falchikov 2007). Instead of serving mainly lawyers' needs, the exams were originally suited to meet the expectations of candidates and those of the general public. Since the relative number of disciplinary cases and complaints did not increase after 2009, when an ever larger group of legal professionals originated from those who joined the profession after the reforms, it is likely that the new requirements at the entry to the profession were adequately set without compromising professionalism. It is noteworthy that of the 39 jurisdictions surveyed by the Organisation for Economic Co-operation and Development (2018), 9 had professional examinations administered by the state jointly with a professional body.

Since disciplinary actions are taken only in cases where no other options remain and the functioning of legal professions rests predominantly on individual self-regulation, group identification, and peer pressure (Boon and Whyte 2019), it seems that additional changes, if any, in regulation of the legal services market should focus on the importance of acquiring ethical skills (professionalization).

Notes

1. Unfortunately, there are no data available on the pass rates at the professional exams administered until 2009 by the bar associations (each of 19 district chambers of legal advisors and 24 district bar councils of advocates separately) to conduct comparisons with the chances of becoming a lawyer immediately after the reform, 2005–2008.
2. See Białowolski and Masior for other approaches (2021).
3. To our knowledge, the National Chamber of Legal Advisors does not write or publish such comprehensive reports. However, the yearly statistics we were interested in are gathered on a local level by the district bar chambers, so the National Chamber of Legal Advisors gathered and aggregated them at our request. We are thankful both to the Polish Bar Council and the National Chamber of Legal Advisors for their valuable input.
4. There are reasonable grounds to assume that the propensity to complain in the Polish society did not change in the period under investigation (from 2000 to 2015). For example, the proportion of Poles who signed a petition in previous year remained constant and stood at 7–9 percent (Czapiński and Panek 2015).
5. Unfortunately, we were not able to obtain data for earlier periods.

References

American Bar Association. 2018. *Model Rules of Professional Conduct.* Washington, DC: American Bar Association. https://www.americanbar .org/groups/professional_responsibility/publications/model_rules_of _professional_conduct/model_rules_of_professional_conduct_table_of _contents/ (accessed December 14, 2021).

Białowolski, Piotr, and Michał Masior. 2021. "Deregulation, Quality and Access—The Case of Legal Professionals in Poland." *Social Policy & Administration* 13(11): 5841.

Bialowolski, Piotr, and Dorota Weziak-Bialowolska. 2021. "What Does It Take to Be a Good Lawyer? The Underpinnings of Success in a Rapidly Growing Legal Market." *Sustainability* 13(11): 1–15.

Boon, Andrew. 2010. "Professionalism under the Legal Services Act 2007." *International Journal of the Legal Profession* 17(3): 195–232.

———. 2014. *The Ethics and Conduct of Lawyers in England and Wales.* Oxford, U.K., and Portland, OR: Hart Publishing.

Boon, Andrew, and Avis Whyte. 2019. "Lawyer Disciplinary Processes: An Empirical Study of Solicitors' Misconduct Cases in England and Wales in 2015." *Legal Studies* 39(3): 455–478.

Boud, David, and Nancy Falchikov. 2007. "Introduction: Assessment for the Longer Term." In *Rethinking Assessment for Higher Education: Learning for the Longer Term*, David Boud and Nancy Falchikov, eds. London: Routledge, pp. 3–13.

Brady, Michael K., and J. Joseph Cronin. 2001. "Some New Thoughts on Conceptualizing Perceived Service Quality: A Hierarchical Approach." *Journal of Marketing* 65(3): 34–49.

Buttle, Francis. 1996. "SERVQUAL: Review, Critique, Research Agenda." *European Journal of Marketing* 30(1): 8–32.

Czapiński, Janusz, and Tomasz Panek, eds. 2015. *Social Diagnosis 2015. Objective and Subjective Quality of Life in Poland.* Council for Social Monitoring. http://www.diagnoza.com/index-en.html (accessed December 14, 2021).

Decker, Christopher, and George Yarrow. 2010. *Understanding the Economic Rationale for Legal Services Regulation.* Oxford, U.K.: Regulatory Policy Institute.

Devlin, Richard F. 2017. "Regulating Lawyers: North American Perspectives and Problematics." *International Lawyer* 50(3): 401–407.

Dewatripont, Mathias, and Jean Tirole. 1999. "Advocates." *Journal of Political Economy* 107(1): 1–39.

Gordon, Tahlia, Rita Shackel, and Steve Mark. 2012. "Regulation of Legal Services in the E-World: A Need to Short Circuit Hot Spots in Ethics and Novel Practices?" *International Journal of the Legal Profession* 19(1): 55–87.

Hirshleifer, Jack, and Evan Osborne. 2001. "Truth, Effort, and the Legal Battle." *Public Choice* 108: 169–195.

Ishida, Kyoko. 2017. "Deterioration or Refinement? Impacts of an Increasing Number of Lawyers on the Lawyer Discipline System in Japan." *International Journal of the Legal Profession* 24(3): 243–257.

Kleiner, Morris M. 2006. *Licensing Occupations: Ensuring Quality or Restricting Competition?* Kalamazoo, Michigan: W.E. Upjohn Institute for Employment Research.

Masior, Michał. 2017. "Analiza wpływu zmiany reguł dostępu do zawodu adwokata i radcy prawnego na jakość usług prawnych." *Współczesne wyzwania w zakresie funkcjonowania przedsiębiorstw. Perspektywa badawcza młodych naukowców*, zredagowane przez, Justyna Szumniak-Samolej, ed. Warszawa: Oficyna Wydawnicza SGH.

Mayson, Stephen. 2016. "Civil Legal Aid: Squaring the (Vicious) Circle." Guildford, England: Legal Services Institute.

———. 2020. *Reforming Legal Services. Regulation beyond the Echo Chambers*. Report of the Independent Review of Legal Services Regulation. London: Centre for Ethics & Law.

Organisation for Economic Co-operation and Development. 2018. "Underlying Data—Sector Indicators of Product Market Regulation." Paris: OECD Publishing.

Ota, S. 2014. "Bengoshi no minjisoshō ni okeru pafōmansu hyōka: hōsō no shitsu no jisshō kenkyū (Assessment of the attorneys' performance in civil litigation: an empirical study on the quality of the legal profession)." *University of Tokyo Law Review* 9: 132–156.

Parasuraman, A., Valarie A. Zeithaml, and Leonard L. Berry. 1985. "A Conceptual Model of Service Quality and Its Implications for Future Research." *Journal of Marketing* 49(4): 41–50.

———. 1988. "SERVQUAL Multiple-item Measuring Perceptions of Service Quality." *Journal of Retailing* 64(1): 12–37.

Ross, H. Laurence. 1980. *Settled Out of Court: The Social Process of Insurance Claims Adjustment*, 2nd ed. New York: Aldine Publishing Co.

Semple, Noel. 2013. "Access to Justice: Is Legal Services Regulation Blocking the Path?" *International Journal of the Legal Profession* 20(3): 267–283.

Stewart, Heather M., Christine A. Hope, and Alan P. Muhlemann. 2000. "Service Quality in the Legal Profession: A Review." *International Journal of Management Reviews* 2(3): 261–285.

Timmons, Edward J., and Robert J. Thornton. 2017. "Licensure or License?

Prospects for Occupational Deregulation." *Labor Law Journal* 68(1): 46–57.

———. 2019. "There and Back Again: The De-Licensing and Re-Licensing of Barbers in Alabama." *British Journal of Industrial Relations* 57(4): 764–790.

6
Restrictions on Health Care Profession Scope of Practice

Do They Help or Harm Patients?

Kihwan Bae
Edward Timmons
West Virginia University,
Knee Center for the Study of Occupational Regulation

WHAT IS SCOPE OF PRACTICE?

Occupational licensing has grown significantly in the United States, especially in the health care services and education industry. According to the Bureau of Labor Statistics (2022), in 2021, more than 40 percent of workers in that industry require a license. Occupational licensing is intended to provide consumer protection from incompetent or unscrupulous purveyors of a service (Kleiner 2015). Although the traditional arguments in support of occupational licensing are strongest in the health care industry, it is less clear why the tasks of medical professionals should be rigidly defined and inflexible, particularly in a rapidly changing environment. Medical service demand increases, technology improves, and the market adapts and changes. It is not fully understood whether limitations on the tasks performed by medical providers are consistent with patients receiving the best quality of service.

Scope of practice (SOP) laws specify what kinds of tasks or functions can be legitimately performed by practitioners in a specific occupation. They determine the boundary of authority for occupations that provide similar services, and frequently stipulate a supervisory or collaborative relationship between physicians and other medical practitioners. As a result, a strict SOP regulation may prevent medical practitioners from working to the full extent of their training and may lead to inefficient labor utilization and contribute to shortfalls in access to care.[1]

In medicine, there are vast differences across states with respect to what nurse practitioners and physician assistants are permitted to do in various settings. Certified nurse midwives and certified registered nurse anesthetists are also facing significant regulation that prevents them from working to the full extent of their training. Patients seeking physical therapists may be forced to see a physician before or soon after receiving treatment. Despite receiving more pharmacology training than most physicians, pharmacists are often limited in the provision of medical services.[2]

We begin this chapter by documenting current issues in SOP regulations and how the regulations vary across states. We then summarize evidence on the effects of liberalizing SOP regulations on health outcomes such as infant mortality, care quality, and emergency room visits. Lastly, we present a roadmap for possible policy reform.

WHAT ARE THE RELEVANT ISSUES IN SOP BY PROFESSION, AND HOW DO STATES DIFFER?

We examine SOP regulations on six medical professions: nurse practitioners (NPs), physician assistants (PAs), certified nurse midwives (CNMs), certified registered nurse anesthetists, physical therapists (PTs), and pharmacists. With specialized education and training, these medical practitioners may have the ability to perform some of the tasks or functions that have been performed by physicians. Moreover, training these practitioners is less costly than training physicians because their education requirements are lower. Therefore, granting these practitioners the authority to practice to the full extent of their training can increase access to medical services and reduce service costs. This approach seems particularly relevant in a rapidly aging society with growing demands for medical services. However, SOP regulations often prohibit practitioners from independently providing medical services, greatly limiting the ability of the providers to fill in gaps in medical care.

Scope of practice regulations are very complex. First, practitioners in different professions have different specialties, so they naturally have different SOP. Next, practitioners in each profession perform several distinct functions that are regulated separately. Indeed, SOP regulations frequently distinguish prescription authority from practice authority. Moreover, the tasks that can be performed legitimately by a professional are regulated at the state level and differ widely across states. Furthermore, for some practitioners, the functions that are permissible are determined at the individual practice level. For some practitioners, whether they can perform a specific function is contingent on function-specific education or licensing requirements. These complexities present additional barriers to the efficient use of the medical workforce.

State regulation grants physicians broad authority to practice medicine based on their own judgment.[3] But most other practitioners, such as NPs and PAs, face limitations on which tasks they can perform without involvement from a physician. Both of those professions appeared in the 1960s in response to the excess demand for primary care physicians in the United States (Timmons 2017). The number of NPs and PAs has gradually increased and is now approaching the number of primary care physicians (Stange 2014). Nurse practitioners are registered nurses who completed specialized graduate education and a nationally administered certification exam to treat common illnesses and prescribe medications. Given their specialty in primary care, broadening their SOP and allowing them to work independently has been suggested as a way to improve care access and reduce care costs (Adams and Markowitz 2018; Kaiser Commission on Medicaid and the Uninsured 2011). Currently, most states recognize NPs as primary care providers, and several states authorize them to practice and prescribe independently from physicians. As a result, NPs help fill gaps in service access in medically underserved areas (Kurtzman et al. 2017). Nevertheless, SOP regulations in many states still require NPs to practice or prescribe under the supervision of or in cooperation with physicians.

Similar to NPs, PAs are equipped with practical knowledge on general medicine and clinical experience through graduate-level education that may qualify them to provide primary care without physician supervision (Adams and Markowitz 2018; Kaiser Commission on Medicaid and the Uninsured 2011). Interestingly, however, PA SOP is determined differently than NP SOP—PAs are permitted to perform any tasks delegated to them by physicians (Stange 2014). In other words, their SOP is determined by physicians at the individual practice level (Scope of Practice Policy 2020a). Accordingly, whether they can prescribe medications—and which types—is also determined at the practice level. This regulatory structure clearly removes the possibility that a PA can independently serve patients in medically underserved areas.

Like NPs, other advanced practice registered nurses also face SOP regulations that limit their independent practice. Certified nurse midwives are registered nurses who completed specialized education and a national certification exam on the birthing process and well-woman gynecological care. Historically, midwifery was first licensed in Illinois in 1877, and many states adopted a similar regulation in the early 1900s (Anderson et al. 2020). Then, nurse-midwifery began in 1925 and evolved to CNMs through the 1960s (Dawley 2003). In 2018, CNMs attended 9.4 percent of total births and 20.1 percent of births from American Indians or Alaska Natives (Centers for Disease Control and Prevention 2019). They have independent practice and prescription authority in most states. However, some states require a collaborative practice agreement or supervision of physicians for the practice of CNMs, and some explicitly require a written protocol on allowable practices as a part of collaboration or supervision, thereby adding significant administrative burdens (Markowitz et al. 2017).

Certified registered nurse anesthetists (CRNAs) are registered nurses who obtained specialized graduate-level training for administering anesthesia and overseeing patient recovery. Nurse anesthetists have been providing patient care for more than 150 years, and CRNAs came into existence in 1956 (American Association of Nurse Anesthetists 2020a). They are the primary provider of anesthesia in rural areas (American Association of Nurse Anesthetists 2020b). Unlike advanced practice registered nurses, CRNAs face a nationwide regulation that significantly limits their SOP. Medicare and Medicaid reimbursement rules specify that a surgeon or anesthesiologist oversee the provision of anesthesia by CRNAs (Dulisse and Cromwell 2010). Since the Centers for Medicare and Medicaid Services (CMS) allowed states to opt out of the requirement in 2001, some states have expanded the SOP of CRNAs; however, most states maintain the CMS requirement, which effectively limits independent practice of CRNAs.

Physical therapists are another profession where tasks are severely limited by SOP regulations. PTs specialize in examining and treating human bodies with physical means and are required to obtain a doctorate degree of physical therapy. The field of physical therapy was established around 1916 with the polio epidemic and World War I (Timmons, Hockenberry, and Durrance 2016). The role of PTs has been limited by physicians for many years by a requirement that patients get a physician's referral before obtaining physical therapy care. Since Nebraska granted direct access authority to PTs in 1957, a growing number of states allow patients to visit PTs without a referral (Timmons, Hockenberry, and Durrance 2016). Despite this trend, most states limit direct access to PTs by stipulating maximum treatment periods before a physician visit is required.[4]

Pharmacists have long been forbidden to prescribe drugs without a physician's order. Given their training in pharmacology and medicine, they have the proper knowledge and skills to prescribe some types of drugs and to provide additional medical service independently from physicians. In this vein, some states allow pharmacists to modify medication regimens from the original prescription either independently or in cooperation with the original prescriber, and some states allow pharmacists to provide hormonal contraceptives (Rodriguez et al. 2020) or smoking cessation aids (Adams and Hudmon 2018). All states allow pharmacists to provide vaccination service to adults (McConeghy and Wing 2016). In 2017, Idaho passed legislation granting pharmacists the broadest SOP in the nation—allowing pharmacists the authority to prescribe medication in several specific instances (Broughel, Haunschild, and Yatsyshina 2020). Most states still limit the role of pharmacists within the physician's prescription order, and many states also impose patient-age limitations on child vaccinations.

Comparison across States by Professions

We now turn to our comparisons of SOP regulations in each state. Because of the previously noted complexities in SOP regulations, there may be alternative measurements on the restrictiveness of a state's SOP regulations. We use publicly available information on SOP regulations that is compiled by professional associations, which closely tracks SOP for the purpose of advocacy and to keep individual members informed of new developments.

Figure 6.1 provides an overview of NP SOP as of June 2021. Twenty-three states and D.C. allow NPs to practice to the full extent of their training.[5] Most of these states grant independent practice authority and independent prescription authority together. In contrast, 27 states still limit the ability of NPs to practice independently from physicians. Among them, 16 states with reduced SOP require a career-long collaborative agreement with physicians, and 11 states with restricted SOP require career-long supervision, delegation, or team management by physicians. In addition, 39 states explicitly recognize NPs as primary care providers, while 11 states and D.C. do not (Scope of Practice Policy 2020b). Considering that NPs are certified based on a national standardized education and exam, the substantial variations in NP SOP across states cannot be justified based on differences in skills or human capital across states.

Unlike NP SOP, PA SOP is determined mostly by physicians. Figure 6.2 illustrates differences in PA SOP as of September 2020. In 37 states and D.C., supervising physicians or clinical teams set the procedures PAs are allowed to perform at the practice level. In the remaining 13 states, SOP is regulated by the state medical board or state laws

Figure 6.1 Scope of Practice for Nurse Practitioners

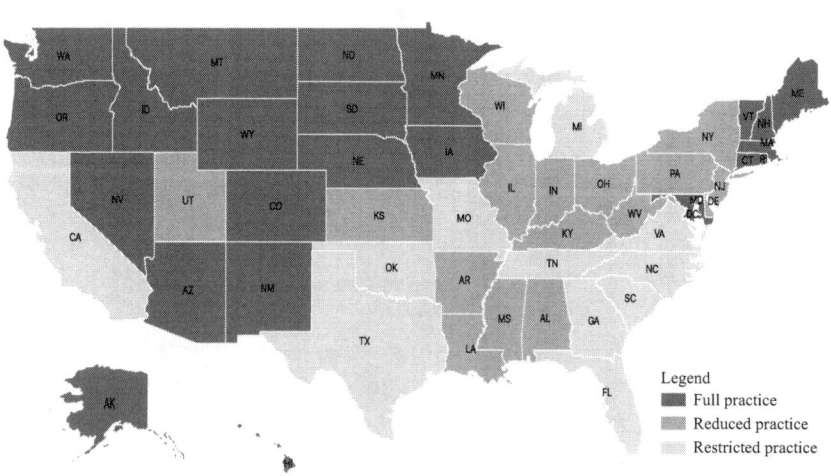

SOURCE: American Association of Nurse Practitioners (2021).

Figure 6.2 Scope of Practice for Physician Assistants

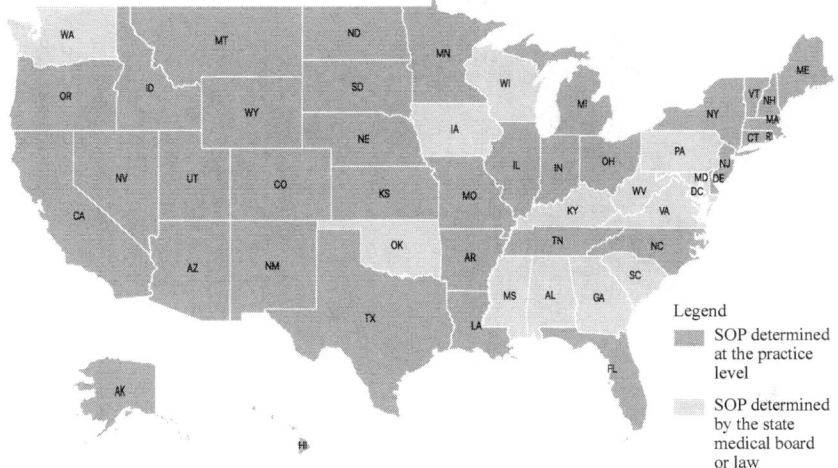

SOURCE: Scope of Practice Policy (2020a).

(Scope of Practice Policy 2020a). Similarly, PA prescription authority is usually determined at the practice level. In addition, several states do not allow PAs to prescribe certain types of controlled substances. It is interesting to note that NPs and PAs may perform similar tasks in clinical teams. SOP determined at the practice level purportedly gives more flexibility to clinical teams than SOP laws (American Association of Physician Assistants 2019). Increased flexibility, however, does not necessarily mean that PAs are allowed to perform to the full extent of their training.

As shown in Figure 6.3, CNMs have independent practice and prescription authority in 27 states and D.C. However, 19 other states require CNMs to perform under a collaborative practice agreement with physicians. A subset of these states requires a collaborative practice agreement for prescription authority only, while other states require an agreement for both practice and prescription. Moreover, the remaining 4 states require direct physician supervision of CNMs, which significantly limits the ability of CNMs to provide care and fill in gaps in care in medically underserved populations.

Figure 6.3 Scope of Practice for Certified Nurse Midwives

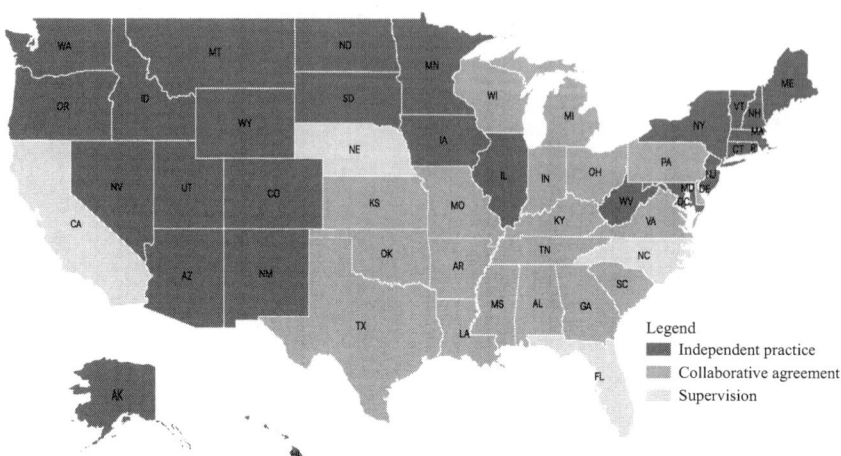

SOURCE: American College of Nurse-Midwives (2018).

Figure 6.4 shows that CRNAs may be able to provide anesthesia independently from physicians in 18 states, all of which opted out of the physician supervision requirement for the CMS. Colorado is in a partial opt-out status, permitting CRNAs to administer anesthesia independently in critical access hospitals and certain rural hospitals. In the remaining 31 states and D.C., CRNAs still need the supervision of a surgeon or anesthesiologist to get Medicaid reimbursements for their practices. This restriction clearly limits CRNA independence and limits their potential to improve access to anesthesia services in rural communities.

Figure 6.5 shows how states compare with respect to patient direct access to physical therapy services. PTs are allowed to treat patients without any limitations and physician referral in 20 states with unrestricted direct access. Twenty-seven states and D.C. require a referral for a certain treatment or limit patients' access time and frequency to PT services. In Alabama, Missouri, and Mississippi, PTs can meet and treat patients after a previous diagnosis or referral by physicians only, or direct access may be permitted only when treating certain patient populations.

Figure 6.4 Scope of Practice for Certified Registered Nurse Anesthetists
(Physician Supervision Requirement for CMS Reimbursement)

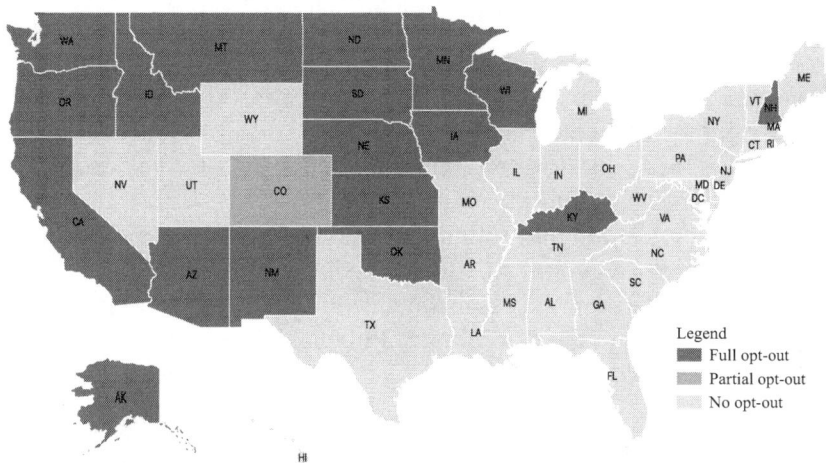

NOTE: Opt-out means CRNAs can obtain CMS reimbursements for their independent
practices without physician oversight.
SOURCE: American Association of Nurse Anesthetists (2020b).

Figure 6.5 Direct Access for Physical Therapists

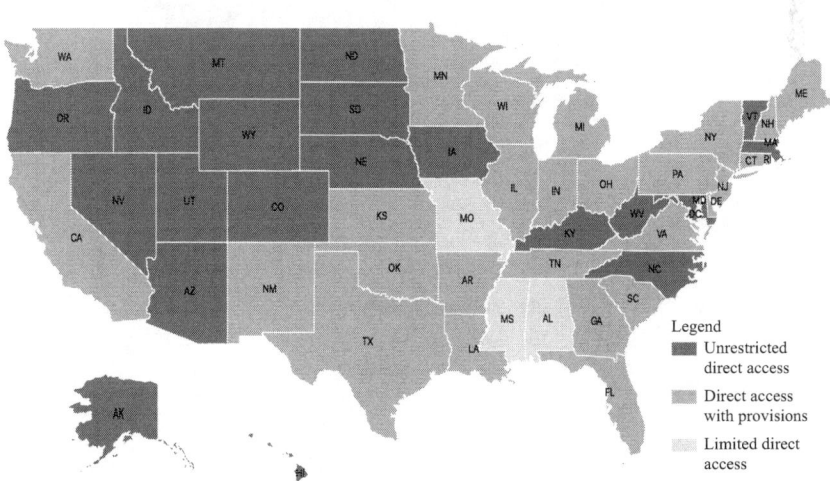

SOURCE: American Physical Therapy Association (2020).

As noted in the previous section, the SOP of pharmacists is quite complex and involves several distinct functions, such as prescription adaptation, vaccination, hormonal contraceptives, and smoking cessation aids. In Figure 6.6, we focus on limitations on pharmacists administering child vaccinations. Twenty-seven states allow pharmacists to provide a vaccination to all children; 20 states and D.C. prohibit pharmacists from administering vaccinations to children under a certain age. Connecticut, Florida, and Vermont do not allow pharmacists to vaccinate children. With respect to other medical services, pharmacists may prescribe smoking cessation aids in 12 states and hormonal contraceptives in 9 states and D.C. Idaho, Indiana, and Maine allow pharmacists to modify medications independently or in cooperation with the original prescriber (Scope of Practice Policy 2020c).

Figure 6.6 Limitations on Pharmacists to Administer Child Vaccination

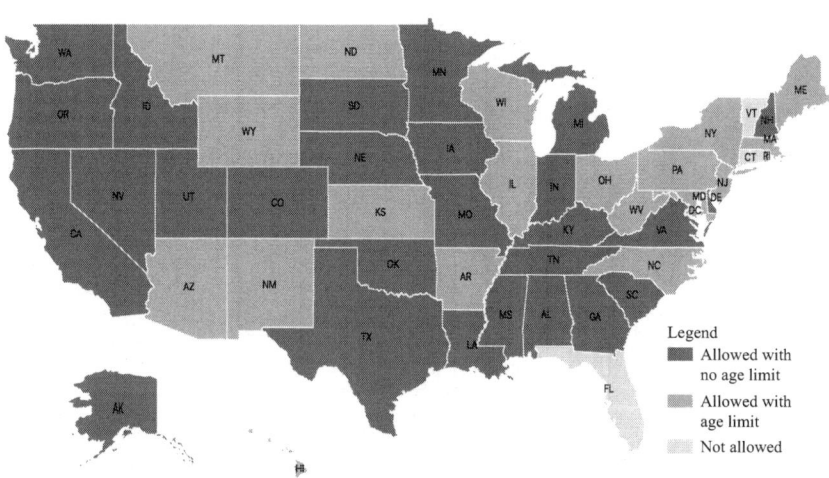

SOURCE: American Pharmacists Association (2019).

Exploring Trends in SOP

In the preceding sections we highlight differences across states with respect to SOP. Are there any common trends? For a systematic correlation analysis, we focus on the full practice authority of the following four occupations: full practice of NPs (Figure 6.1), independent practice of CNMs (Figure 6.3), CMS opt-out for CRNAs (Figure 6.4), and unlimited direct access of PTs (Figure 6.5). As summarized in Figure 6.7, 47 percent of all 50 states plus D.C. grant NPs full practice authority, 55 percent CNMs, 35 percent CRNAs, and 39 percent PTs.

Figure 6.7 Full Practice Authority

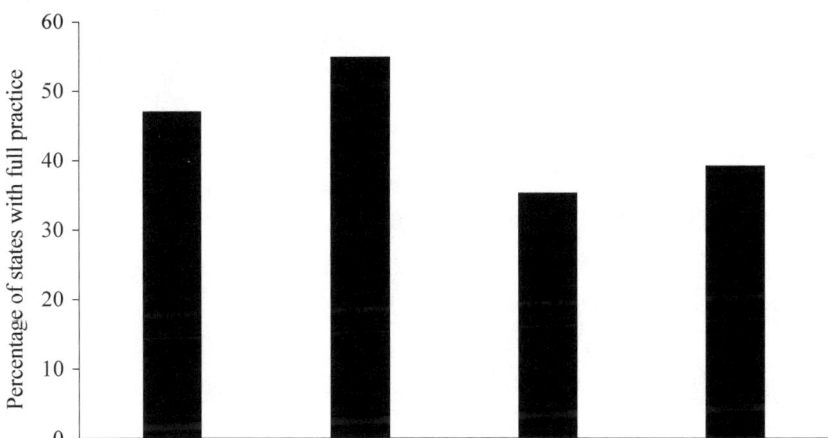

SOURCE: Authors' calculation based on data from American Association of Nurse Practitioners (2021), American College of Nurse-Midwives (2018), American Association of Nurse Anesthetists (2020b), American Physical Therapy Association (2020).

Our first finding is that states granting full practice authority to an occupation tend to give it to other occupations. Table 6.1 shows that the full practice authority of NPs, CNMs, CRNAs, and PTs is positively correlated with each other. NP and CNM full practice authority have the highest correlation (0.776) and is statistically significant at the 0.1 percent level. PT full practice authority also has a strong positive correlation with NP and CNM full practice authority.

Turning our attention to geography, we find that there are clear geographic differences in full practice authority: states in the western region are the most likely to grant full practice authority to the four

Table 6.1 Correlation in Full Practice Authority between Professions

	NP	CNM	CRNA	PT
NP	1.000	0.776***	0.372**	0.530***
CNM	0.776***	1.000	0.175	0.486***
CRNA	0.372**	0.175	1.000	0.247*
PT	0.530***	0.486***	0.247*	1.000

NOTE: * significant at the 0.10 level; ** significant at the 0.01 level; *** significant at the 0.001 level. Pearson correlation coefficients.

SOURCE: Authors' calculations based on data from American Association of Nurse Practitioners (2021), American College of Nurse-Midwives (2018), American Association of Nurse Anesthetists (2020b), American Physical Therapy Association (2020).

occupations, while states in the southern region are the least likely (Figure 6.8). Interestingly, the northeast region generally grants full practice to NPs and CNMs but is more restrictive for CRNAs and PTs.

Figure 6.8 Full Practice Authority by Census Regions

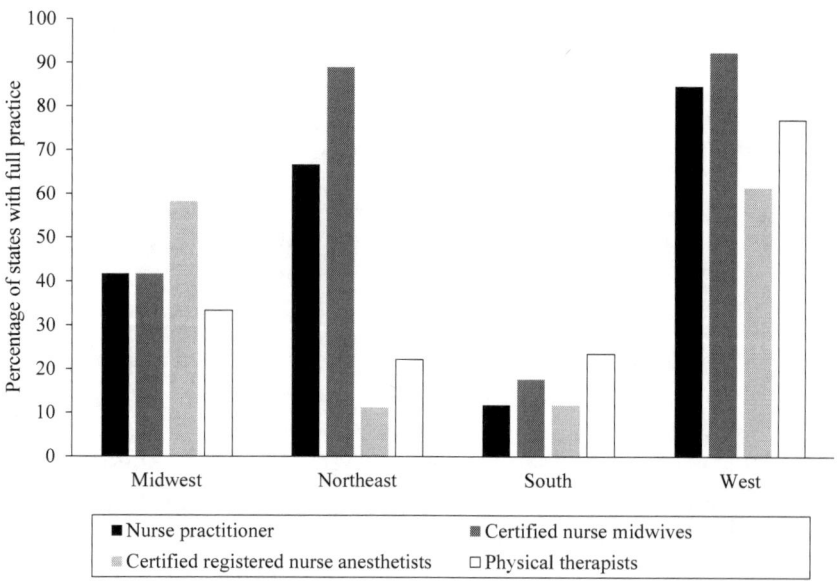

SOURCE: Authors' calculations based on data from American Association of Nurse Practitioners (2021), American College of Nurse-Midwives (2018), American Association of Nurse Anesthetists (2020b), American Physical Therapy Association (2020).

Table 6.2 takes a closer look at geographic concentration of full practice authority at the census division level. Interesting regional differences emerge from this comparison. For example, in the Midwest region, the majority of states in the west north central division allow full practice to all four occupations, whereas very few states in the east north central division grant the same freedom to practice. In the northeast region, all states in the New England division allow NP full practice, but none in the middle Atlantic division grant this permission. It is also worth noting that not a single state in the east and west south central divisions in the southern region authorize NPs and CNMs to practice to the full extent of their training.

In summary, we provide empirical evidence on the correlation and diffusion of SOP expansion across occupations and states and observe that the similarity between occupations and geographic proximity

Table 6.2 Full Practice Authority by Census Divisions

Region	Division (member states)	NP	CNM	CRNA	PT
Midwest	East north central (IL, IN, MI, OH, WI)	0.0	20.0	20.0	0.0
	West north central (IA, KS, MN, MO, NE, ND, SD)	71.4	57.1	85.7	57.1
Northeast	Middle Atlantic (NJ, NY, PA)	0.0	66.7	0.0	0.0
	New England (CT, ME, MA, NH, RI, VT)	100.0	100.0	16.7	33.3
South	East south central (AL, KY, MS, TN)	0.0	0.0	25.0	25.0
	South Atlantic (DE, DC, FL, GA, MD, NC, SC, VA, WV)	22.2	33.3	0.0	33.3
	West south central (AR, LA, OK, TX)	0.0	0.0	25.0	0.0
West	Mountain (AZ, CO, ID, MT, NV, NM, UT, WY)	87.5	100.0	50.0	87.5
	Pacific (AK, CA, HI, OR, WA)	80.0	80.0	80.0	60.0

NOTE: Percentage of states with full practice authority for NMs, CNMs, CRNAs, and PTs by census divisions.

SOURCE: Authors' calculations based on data from American Association of Nurse Practitioners (2021), American College of Nurse-Midwives (2018), American Association of Nurse Anesthetists (2020b), American Physical Therapy Association (2020).

between states play an important role in SOP reforms. This pattern implies that the state-level regulatory environment or geography that is independent from occupation-specific factors may be key for determining SOP. If SOP is indeed heavily affected by political factors rather than practitioner training and competency, it is more likely that the regulation may not benefit patients but just strengthen special interests (Friedman 1962). To further explore this hypothesis, in the next section we summarize the existing empirical evidence of the effects of SOP differences on quality.

WHAT IS THE EVIDENCE?

As our summary of the literature will show, there is accumulating evidence that restricted SOP does not improve the quality of medical service, but instead limits access to medical services. In fact, some studies demonstrate that the relaxation of SOP regulations results in improved health outcomes. These findings are consistent across studies with a variety of health outcomes such as self-reported health, regular checkups, office visits, hospitalizations, mortality, infant health, and birth outcomes. The findings are also robust to alternative measurements for SOP. Given the complexities in SOP regulations, studies tend to focus on whether a state allows fully independent practice and prescription authority without any physician involvement. Other studies focus exclusively on independent prescription authority instead, while other studies use indexes that measure overall restrictiveness of SOP regulations. Furthermore, studies using policy variations across states and those using within-state variations over time reach a similar conclusion—granting independent practice authority to health care service providers does not reduce the quality of care.

As shown in Table 6.3, the largest number of existing studies on SOP and service quality focus on NPs. Traczynski and Udalova (2018) find that NP independent practice improves self-reported health status and raises the frequency of routine checkups. The authors also find evidence that NP independence reduces indirect costs relating to appointments or travel and increases patient-reported care quality. They classify a state's NP practice environment as independent if the state permits

Table 6.3 SOP Expansion and Health Outcomes

Study	Profession	SOP measure	Effects on health outcomes
Traczynski and Udalova (2018)	NPs	Both practice and prescription authority	NP independence increases the frequency of routine checkups and the fraction of people whose self-reported health status is excellent.
Alexander and Schnell (2019)	NPs	Prescription authority	NP independent prescription reduces the number of days in poor mental health (self-reported) and mental health-related mortality rates.
Kleiner et al. (2016)	NPs	Prescription authority	NP restricted prescription does not improve infant mortality rates but increases service prices of well-child visits.
Kurtzman et al. (2017)	NPs	Practice and prescription authority	NP independence does not reduce service quality such as depression treatment but increases service utilization such as counseling and medication.
Perloff et al. (2017)	NPs	Practice and prescription authority	NP restricted practice or prescription does not improve quality of primary care such as chronic disease management and cancer screening.
Markowitz et al. (2017)	CNMs	Practice and prescription authority	CNM independence does not change maternal and infant health comes but raises CNM-attended births and lowers labor inductions and C-sections.
Yang, Attanasio, and Kozhimannil (2016)	CNMs	Practice authority	CNM independence increases CNM-attended births and reduces C-sections, preterm births, and low-weight births.
Dulisse and Cromwell (2010)	CRNAs	CMS physician supervision requirement	CRNA independence does not increase surgical inpatient mortality rates and complication rates from anesthesia.

both independent practice and prescriptive authority. They study the effects of policy changes in NP independence in eight states. Their sample is individuals in the Medical Expenditure Panel Survey Adult Self-Administered Questionnaire data from 1999–2012.

In a similarly designed study, Alexander and Schnell (2019) find that NP independent prescription authority improves self-reported mental health outcomes. Moreover, they find that the benefits from independent NPs are concentrated in medically underserved areas. In these underserved areas, NP independent prescriptive authority reduces mental health–related mortality rates as well as increases self-reported mental health. They measure NP independent prescription authority from 1990 to 2014 based on the NP's legislative updates, correspondence with state nursing boards, and state statutes. Their study examines the effects of policy changes in prescription authority in 18 states. They use county-quarter-level mortality data from the U.S. mortality files to measure mental health–related mortality rates and data from the Behavioral Risk Factor Surveillance System to measure self-reported mental health.

Exploring the effect of NP prescriptive authority on a variety of outcomes, Kleiner et al. (2016) find that restricted NP autonomy does not improve infant mortality rates but raises service prices. The authors classify NP prescription autonomy into three categories: independent, supervised or delegated, and limited. They look into the effects of state policy changes with five-year county-level infant mortality rates data in 1999–2004 and individual insurance claims data in 2005–2010.

Two other studies that focus on health outcomes for medically underserved communities or populations are also worth noting. Kurtzman et al. (2017) have shown that NP full independence does not reduce quality of care relating to smoking cessation, depression treatment, and statin prescriptions at community health centers. Their study defines whether NPs have full independence with respect to practice and prescriptive privilege based on the ratings provided in *Nurse Practitioner* magazine. The authors compare health outcomes between states with full independence and those without. Their sample is the National Ambulatory Medical Care Survey Community Health Center subsample in 2006–2011.

Similarly, Perloff et al. (2017) document that restrictive NP SOP does not improve quality of primary care relating to chronic diseases, preventable hospitalizations, adverse outcomes, and cancer screening of Medicare beneficiaries. The authors separate states into three categories of NP independence: full, reduced, and restricted authority. They compare health outcomes in the three groups of states. Their sample consists of aged and disabled beneficiaries in Medicare claims data in 2012–2013.

Several studies have examined the effects of CNM SOP on maternal and infant health outcomes. Markowitz et al. (2017) show that CNM SOP does not affect maternal health behaviors during pregnancy. The authors also find that states with less restrictive CNM SOP regulations have fewer induced labors and C-sections, slightly longer gestation ages, and larger newborn weights than states with more restrictive SOP regulations. Based on the Nurse Practitioner's legislative updates and state statutes, they categorize SOP barriers in practice and prescription authority into four different levels: none, low, moderate, and high. They examine the effects of state policy changes with birth certificate data from the Centers for Disease Control's National Vital Statistics System for 1994–2013.

Yang, Attanasio, and Kozhimannil (2016) find similar results using the National Center for Health Statistics Natality Detail File data for 2009–2011. Their study shows that autonomous CNM practice reduces the likelihood of C-section, preterm birth, and low-weight birth. They distinguish states with autonomous midwifery practice from those subject to supervisory or collaborative agreement, based on LexisNexis legal research, and compare the outcomes between the two groups.

Another noteworthy study examines how removing physician supervision requirements affects quality of care provided by CRNAs. Dulisse and Cromwell (2010) find that states allowing CRNAs to administer anesthesia independently did not experience an increase in mortality or complication rates. The authors study the effects of policy changes in 14 states immediately after the CMS allowed states to opt out of physician supervision requirements in 2001. They use the 5 percent Medicare Inpatient (Part A) and Carrier (Part B) Medicare limited data set files for 1999–2005.

To summarize the existing literature, studies on SOP changes and the implications for the quality of care concentrate on advanced practice registered nurses, including NPs, CNMs, and CRNAs. The current focus on advanced practice registered nurses may be a direct result of the important roles they can play as primary care providers in many states amid the ongoing shortage of physicians. In contrast, it is largely an unexplored topic of how SOP regulations in other professions affect service quality in the United States. A handful of studies focusing on European countries have documented that patients obtaining PT services without physician referral have higher satisfaction and better discharge outcomes than patients referred by physicians (Holdsworth and Webster 2004; Ojha, Snyder, and Davenport 2014; Webster et al. 2008).

In addition to research that estimates how SOP affects health outcomes, several studies have also examined how differences in regulation affect the utilization or costs of medical services. This strand of the existing literature does not look directly into care quality, but it is very likely that improvements in access and reductions in prices will be correlated with improved health outcomes. Studies focusing on NPs have shown that their full independence increases office visits (Stange 2014), the provision of counseling and medication in community health centers (Kurtzman et al. 2017), and medication prescriptions in retail clinics (Spetz et al. 2013) and also decreases hospitalization rates (Oliver et al. 2014) and the price of well-child visits (Kleiner et al. 2016). Turning to CNMs, studies have found that more consumers choose CNM delivery when their practice becomes more autonomous (Markowitz et al. 2017; Yang, Attanasio, and Kozhimannil 2016). Studies on PAs have documented mixed results as to whether their independent prescription authority reduces office visits (Stange 2014) and lowers the cost of outpatient claims per Medicaid beneficiary (Timmons 2017). Regarding pharmacists, studies have shown that allowing influenza vaccinations in community pharmacies increases per-capita influenza vaccine pharmacy prescriptions (e.g., McConeghy and Wing 2016), and pharmacists tend to prescribe hormonal contraceptives over longer time intervals than clinicians (Rodriguez et al. 2020). Taken together, fully granting independent authority to medical providers tends to increase care utilization and reduce service prices, and this likely also improves patient health outcomes. Our survey of the literature suggests that expanding medical provider SOP improves the quality of care delivered to patients. Nonetheless, we observe several possibilities for improving research on SOP and service quality. First, there is still disagreement on the classification of SOP regulation used by researchers. It is uncertain which aspect of NP SOP is most crucial: independent practice authority or independent prescription authority.[6] Moreover, differences in state regulations make it hard to devise a single objective measurement of SOP. In addition, studies on SOP and service quality have used health outcomes, an arguably indirect measurement of service quality. Studies with more direct measurements of quality, such as a procedural outcome or malpractice premiums, may be able to fill the research gap. Finally, as noted in our review, there are many professions where the connection between medical SOP and quality remains largely unexplored. Perhaps as more time passes and more data become available, future research can help fill in these existing gaps in the literature.

COVID-19 WAIVERS AND A ROADMAP FOR REFORM

Our summary of the existing literature on how the expansion of SOP affects the quality of care yields the following stylized fact: granting health care providers—most notably advanced practice registered nurses—the ability to work independently has no measurable negative affect on health outcomes. If there is an effect on quality, the effect seems to be more positive than negative. The policy implications are quite clear. States that currently limit providers from practicing to the full extent of their medical training—which tend to be concentrated in the South— should remove these stringent regulations.

The onset of COVID-19 has highlighted some of the existing limitations in the provision of health care. Hospitals in early hotspots like New York City and New Orleans struggled to provide care to patients as a result of rigidity in health care personnel supply. New York Governor Andrew Cuomo made a public plea for doctors and nurses to come to New York City and help fill in gaps in the provision of care (CBS News 2020). Early in the crisis, the ability of NPs to fulfill their potential was no doubt limited by existing New York law. Although experienced NPs (with 3,600 hours or more of clinical practice) can work independently of physicians, more inexperienced NPs must work collaboratively with physicians (Poghosyan, Norful, and Laugesen 2018)

Recognizing the need for added flexibility, Governor Cuomo issued an executive order on March 23, 2020, granting NPs the authority to practice independently (New York State 2020). Similar temporary waivers were also granted to PAs and CRNAs. Several other states temporarily expanded medical provider SOP to add frontline capacity for treating COVID-19 patients and to also make sure that patients suffering from other ailments and diseases had access to care (Bayne, Norris, and Timmons 2020).

Moreover, the federal government declared emergency rules shortly after the pandemic began to expand the SOP of medical practitioners. On March 17, 2020, the Department of Health and Human Services issued an amendment to override state restrictions on pharmacist-administered vaccination on children over age three (U.S. Department of Health and Human Services 2020). The CMS temporarily suspended physician supervision requirements for CRNAs on March 30. The agency also relaxed rules on physician delegation to and supervision of NPs and PAs in critical access hospitals, federally qualified health centers, and long-term care facilities (Centers for Medicare and Medicaid Services 2020).

In a crisis, state governors and legislators and federal agencies responded quickly and often granted medical providers more independence and broader SOP. As more data become available, it will be interesting to uncover the effects that these temporary waivers had on the quality of care delivered. An early comparison of Ohio and Illinois, two states that did not expand NP SOP, with surrounding Midwest states that granted waivers suggests that COVID-19 deaths were reduced by 10 cases per day in the states that granted temporary waivers (Chung 2020).

Will state policymakers and federal agencies eliminate the temporary waivers after the COVID-19 pandemic ends? Or will there be a recognition that perhaps the restrictions were never in the patients' best interest? Perhaps a renewed push to expand SOP for medical personnel will begin in earnest in coming years. The crisis has created an interesting opportunity for researchers and policymakers alike.

CONCLUSION

In this chapter, we examined how the SOP of health service professionals varies across states. We surveyed the existing literature on the effects of expanding SOP on the quality of care received by patients.

There are noticeable variations in the SOP of the same occupation across states, but positive correlations in the SOP expansion across different occupations in the same state. States in Pacific, Mountain, and West North Central divisions are ahead of other states in granting the full practice authority to health service professionals, while states in the South are way behind. Much of the literature on the SOP and the quality of care focuses on advanced practice registered nurses: NPs, CNMs, and CRNAs. Although the literature has some limitations, there is an emerging consensus: allowing medical practitioners to work independently from physicians does not reduce the quality of care but rather appears to improve the quality of care with no measurable influence on prices. Despite this, regulatory reforms on the SOP are often crippled by professionals who may benefit from existing regulations.

More research is needed on this important empirical question, particularly when it comes to PT direct access and expanding the SOP of pharmacists. The COVID-19 pandemic has provided both researchers and policymakers with an opportunity to further investigate the implications of this important health policy question.

Notes

1. Kleiner (2016) provides a survey of literature on how SOP affects wages and employment of various health care occupations. Adams and Markowitz (2018) survey literature on how SOP of advanced practice registered nurses and physician assistants affects employment, service price, quality, and utilization. Two recent papers examine the effects of licensing on service quality: Farronato et al. (2020) show that licensing of home repair contractors does not improve the service quality measured by consumer satisfaction, while Anderson et al. (2020) demonstrate that midwife licensing reduced maternal and infant mortality between 1900 and 1940. Our focus in this chapter is specifically how SOP of medical providers affects health outcome as a measure of medical service quality.

2. Similar issues exist in the practice of dentistry, with dental hygienists and dental assistants serving a regimented and subordinate role (Chen, Meyerhoefer, and Timmons 2020). As of July 2019, only 13 states permit dental therapists to practice either statewide or within tribal lands although they are much more prevalent outside of the United States (American Dental Hygienists' Association 2019).

3. To receive authorization to perform surgery, physicians must obtain the relevant American Board of Medical Specialties certification and obtain operating room privileges from the hospital treating the patient.

4. There are at least two occupations whose tasks overlap those of physical thera-

pists or physicians: occupational therapists and chiropractors. This book chapter does not deal with issues in these occupations. See Cai and Kleiner (2020) for occupational therapists and Timmons, Hockenberry, and Durrance (2016) for chiropractors.

5. Delaware became the twenty-fourth state to recognize the full practice authority in August 2021 (Campaign for Action 2021).
6. See McMichael and Markowitz (2020) for a recent attempt toward a uniform classification of NP SOP.

References

Adams, Alex J, and Karen Suchanek Hudmon. 2018. "Pharmacist Prescriptive Authority for Smoking Cessation Medications in the United States." *Journal of the American Pharmacists Association* 58(3): 253–257.

Adams, E. Kathleen, and Sara Markowitz. 2018. "Improving Efficiency in the Health-Care System: Removing Anticompetitive Barriers for Advanced Practice Registered Nurses and Physician Assistants." Policy Proposal 2018-08. Washington, DC: The Hamilton Project.

Alexander, Diane, and Molly Schnell. 2019. "Just What the Nurse Practitioner Ordered: Independent Prescriptive Authority and Population Mental Health." *Journal of Health Economics* 66: 145–162.

American Association of Nurse Anesthetists. 2020a. "Certified Registered Nurse Anesthetists Fact Sheet." Park Ridge, IL: American Association of Nurse Anesthetists.

———. 2020b. "Fact Sheet Concerning State Opt-Outs And November 13, 2001 CMS Rule." Park Ridge, IL: American Association of Nurse Anesthetists.

American Association of Nurse Practitioners. 2021. "State Practice Environment." (Updated: 1/1/2021). Austin. TX: American Association of Nurse Practitioners. https://www.aanp.org/advocacy/state/state-practice-environment (accessed February 17, 2021).

American Association of Physician Assistants. 2019. "PA Scope of Practice." Alexandria, VA: American Association of Physician Assistants. https://www.aapa.org/wp-content/uploads/2017/01/Issue-brief_Scope-of-Practice_0117-1.pdf (accessed September 15, 2020).

American College of Nurse-Midwives. 2018. "Practice Environments for Certified Nurse-Midwives as of June 2018." Silver Spring, MD: American College of Nurse-Midwives. https://www.midwife.org/acnm/files/cclibrary files/filename/000000007539/practice%20enviro%20map.jpg (accessed September 15, 2020).

American Dental Hygienists' Association. 2019. "Expanding Access to Care through Dental Therapy." Chicago: American Dental Hygienists' Association. https://www.adha.org/resources-docs/Expanding_Access_to_Dental _Therapy.pdf (accessed September 15, 2020).

American Pharmacists Association. 2019. Washington, DC: American Pharmacists Association. Pharmacist Administered Vaccines. (Updated January 2019.) https://media.pharmacist.com/practice/IZ_Authority_012019.pdf (accessed September 15, 2020).

American Physical Therapy Association. 2020. "Levels of Patient Access to Physical Therapist Services in the U.S." https://www.apta.org/contenta ssets/4daf765978464a948505c2f115c90f55/apta-direct-access-by-state -august2020.pdf (accessed September 15, 2020).

Anderson, D. Mark, Ryan Brown, Krewin Kofi Charles, and Danel I. Rees. 2020. "Occupational Licensing and Maternal Health: Evidence from Early Midwifery Laws." *Journal of Political Economy* 128(11): 4337–4383.

Bayne, Ethan, Conor Norris, and Edwards Timmons. 2020. "A Primer on Emergency Occupational Licensing Reforms for Combating COVID-19." Policy brief. Arlington, VA: Mercatus Center, George Mason University.

Broughel, James, Philip Haunschild, and Yuliya Yatsyshina. 2020. "Reforming the Practice of Pharmacy: Observations from Idaho." Arlington, VA: Mercatus Center, George Mason University.

Bureau of Labor Statistics. 2022. *Data on Certifications and Licenses.* Washington, DC: Bureau of Labor Statistics. https://www.bls.gov/cps/ certifications-and-licenses.htm (accessed March 2022).

Cai, Jing, and Morris M. Kleiner. 2020. "The Labor Market Consequences of Regulating Similar Occupations: The Licensing of Occupational and Physical Therapists." *Journal of Labor Research* 41(4): 352–381.

Campaign for Action. 2021. *Delaware Becomes 24th State to Recognize Full Practice Authority for APRNs.* August 5, 2021. https://campaignforaction .org/delaware-recognizes-aprn-full-practice-authority/ (accessed March, 2022).

CBS News. 2020. *Coronavirus updates from March 30, 2020.* https://www .cbsnews.com/live-updates/coronavirus-disease-covid-19-latest-news -2020-03-30/ (accessed September 15, 2020).

Centers for Disease Control and Prevention. 2019. "Births: Final Data for 2018." *National Vital Statistics Reports* 68(13): 1–47.

Centers for Medicare and Medicaid Services. 2020. *COVID-19 Emergency Declaration Blanket Waivers for Health Care Providers.* https://www.cms .gov/files/document/summary-covid-19-emergency-declaration-waivers .pdf (accessed September 15, 2020).

Chen, Jie, Chad D. Meyerhoefer, and Edward J. Timmons. 2020. "The Effects of Dental Hygienist Autonomy on Dental Care Utilization." Working Paper No. 2020.011. Logan, UT: Center for Growth and Opportunity at Utah State University.

Chung W., Bobby. 2020. "The Impact of Relaxing Nurse Practitioner Licensing to Reduce COVID Mortality: Evidence from the Midwest." Park Ridge, IL: Project for Middle Class Renewal, Labor & Employment Relations, University of Illinois.

Dawley, Katy. 2003. "Origins of Nurse-Midwifery in the United States and Its Expansion in the 1940s." *Journal of Midwifery & Women's Health* 48(2): 86–95.

Dulisse, Brian, and Jerry Cromwell. 2010. "No Harm Found When Nurse Anesthetists Work without Supervision by Physicians." *Health Affairs* 29(8): 1469–1475.

Farronato, Chiara, Bradley Larsen, Andrey Fradkin, and Erik Brynjolfsson. 2020. "Consumer Protection in an Online World: An Analysis of Occupational Licensing." NBER Working Paper No. 26601. Cambridge, MA: National Bureau of Economic Research.

Friedman, Milton. 1962. *Capitalism and Freedom.* Chicago: Chicago University Press.

Holdsworth, Lesley K., and Valerie S. Webster. 2004. "Direct Access to Physiotherapy in Primary Care: Now?—And into the Future?" *Physiotherapy* 90(2): 64–72.

Kaiser Commission on Medicaid and the Uninsured. 2011. "Improving Access to Adult Primary Care in Medicaid: Exploring the Potential Role of Nurse Practitioners and Physician Assistants." https://www.kff.org/wp-content/uploads/2013/01/8167.pdf (accessed September 15, 2020).

Kleiner, Morris M. 2015. *Guild-Ridden Labor Markets: The Curious Case of Occupational Licensing.* Kalamazoo, MI: W.E. Upjohn Institute for Employment.

———. 2016. "Battling over Jobs: Occupational Licensing in Health Care." *American Economic Review: Papers & Proceedings* 106(5): 165–170.

Kleiner, Morris M., Allison Marier, Kyoung Won Park, and Coady Wing. 2016. "Relaxing Occupational Licensing Requirements: Analyzing Wages and Prices for a Medical Service." *Journal of Law and Economics* 59(2): 261–291.

Kurtzman, Ellen T., Burt S. Barnow, Jean E. Johnson, Samuel J. Simmens, Donna Lind Infeld, and Fitzhugh Mullan. 2017. "Does the Regulatory Environment Affect Nurse Practitioners' Patterns of Practice or Quality of Care in Health Centers?" *Health Services Research* 52: 437–458.

Markowitz, Sara, E. Kathleen Adams, Mary Jane Lewitt, and Anne L. Dunlop. 2017. "Competitive Effects of Scope of Practice Restrictions: Public Health or Public Harm?" *Journal of Health Economics* 55: 201–218.

McConeghy, Kevin W., and Coady Wing. 2016. "A National Examination of Pharmacy-Based Immunization Statutes and Their Association with Influenza Vaccinations and Preventive Health." *Vaccine* 34(30): 3463–3468.

McMichael, Benjamin J., and Sara Markowitz. 2020. "Toward a Uniform Classification of Nurse Practitioner Scope of Practice Laws." NBER Working Paper No. 28192 (Revised April 2021). Cambridge, MA: National Bureau of Economic Research.

New York State. 2020. *Excecutive Order No. 202.10: Continuing Temporary Suspension and Modification of Laws Relating to the Disaster Emergency.* March 23. https://www.governor.ny.gov/news/no-20210-continuing -temporary-suspension-and-modification-laws-relating-disaster-emergency (accessed September 15, 2020).

Ojha, Heidi A., Rachel S. Snyder, and Todd E. Davenport. 2014. "Direct Access Compared with Referred Physical Therapy Episodes of Care: A Systematic Review." *Physical Therapy* 94(1): 14–30.

Oliver, Gina M., Lila Pennington, Sara Revelle, and Marilyn Rantz. 2014. "Impact of Nurse Practitioners on Health Outcomes of Medicare and Medicaid Patients." *Nursing Outlook* 62(6): 440–447.

Perloff, Jennifer, Sean Clarke, Catherine M. DesRoches, Monica O'Reilly-Jacob, and Peter Buerhaus. 2017. "Association of State-Level Restrictions in Nurse Practitioner Scope of Practice with the Quality of Primary Care Provided to Medicare Beneficiaries." *Medical Care Research and Review* 76(5): 597–626.

Poghosyan, Lusine, Allison A. Norful, and Miriam J. Laugesen. 2018. "Removing Restrictions on Nurse Practitioners' Scope of Practice in New York State: Physicians' and Nurse Practitioners' Perspectives." *Journal of the American Association of Nurse Practitioner* 30(6): 354–360.

Rodriguez, Maria I., Alison B. Edelman, Megan Skye, Lorinda Anderson, and Blair G. Darney. 2020. "Association of Pharmacist Prescription with Dispensed Duration of Hormonal Contraception." *JAMA Network Open* 3(5): e205252.

Scope of Practice Policy. 2020a. *Physician Assistants Overview.* http://scope ofpracticepolicy.org/practitioners/physician-assistants/ (accessed September 15, 2020).

———. 2020b. *Nurse Practitioners Overview.* http://scopeofpracticepolicy .org/practitioners/nurse-practitioners/ (accessed September 15, 2020).

———. 2020c. *Pharmacists Overview.* http://scopeofpracticepolicy.org/ practitioners/pharmacists/ (accessed September 15, 2020).

Spetz, Joanne, Stephen T. Parente, Robert J. Town, and Dawn Bazarko. 2013. "Scope-of-Practice Laws for Nurse Practitioners Limit Cost Savings That Can Be Achieved in Retail Clinics." *Health Affairs* 32(11): 1977–1984.

Stange, Kevin. 2014. "How Does Provider Supply and Regulation Influence Health Care Markets? Evidence from Nurse Practitioners and Physician Assistants." *Journal of Health Economics* 33: 1–27.

Timmons, Edward J., Jason M. Hockenberry, and Christine Piette Durrance. 2016. "More Battles among Licensed Occupations: Estimating the Effects of Scope of Practice and Direct Access on the Chiropractic, Physical Therapist, and Physician Labor Market." Arlington, VA: Mercatus Center, George Mason University.

Timmons, Edward Joseph. 2017. "The Effects of Expanded Nurse Practitioner and Physician Assistant Scope of Practice on the Cost of Medicaid Patient Care." *Health Policy* 121(2): 189–196.

Traczynski, Jeffrey, and Victoria Udalova. 2018. "Nurse Practitioner Independence, Health Care Utilization, and Health Outcomes." *Journal of Health Economics* 58: 90–109.

U.S. Department of Health and Human Services. 2020. *Third Amendment to Declaration Under the Public Readiness and Emergency Preparedness Act for Medical Countermeasures Against COVID-19.* Washington, DC: U.S. Department of Health and Human Services.

Webster, Valerie S., Lesley K. Holdsworth, Angus K. McFadyen, Helen Little, and Scottish Physiotherapy Self Referral Study Group. 2008. "Self-Referral, Access and Physiotherapy: Patients' Knowledge and Attitudes—Results of a National Trial." *Physiotherapy* 94(2): 141–149.

Yang, Y. Tony, Laura B. Attanasio, and Katy B. Kozhimannil. 2016. "State Scope of Practice Laws, Nurse-Midwifery Workforce, and Childbirth Procedures and Outcomes." *Women's Health Issues* 26(3): 262–267.

7

Testing Licensing and Consumer Satisfaction for Beauty Services in the United States

Darwyyn Deyo
San José State University

Occupational licensing varies widely in the United States, with some occupations heavily licensed in one state and not licensed at all in others. The barriers to labor market entry created by licensing are often defended on the grounds of protecting public health and safety. However, because licensing is required for a multitude of occupations, it becomes more difficult to determine whether licensing achieves its intended objectives. Public health and safety also may be framed as quality, where licensing requirements protect consumers from dishonest or unqualified businesses. Consumer satisfaction, as measured through consumer ratings, provides a window into understanding the link between licensing and quality. This chapter examines licensing and quality for occupations in the beauty services industry using publicly available ratings data in the United States.

This chapter adds to the literature by examining licensing's effect on quality in two occupations related to beauty services: makeup artists and shampooers. Importantly, these occupations are not licensed in every state. This policy variation means we can study the effect of having more or fewer licensing requirements, such as the amount of licensing fees or licensing exams, and the effect of having licensing at all. Studying the depth of licensing is helpful when considering the effect of increasing (or decreasing) specific requirements, whereas studying the breadth of licensing is helpful when considering the effect of passing (or repealing) different licensing requirements.

To study the effect of licensing, I compare the ratings of businesses in licensed occupations (makeup artists and shampooers) with the ratings for an interesting but comparable unlicensed occupation (pet groomers). Pet groomers also shampoo, cut, style, and alter their clients' appearance. Pet groomers may work with dogs, cats, other household pets, and even larger animals. Importantly, the pet has a proxy for reporting quality in the form of the person who paid for the pet grooming. Pet grooming certification is available in most states, but the occupation is not licensed in any of the states in this study. I use the publicly available business ratings from the Yelp Open Dataset and the License to Work licensing dataset (Carpenter et al. 2017) to estimate the effect of licensing on quality across these occupations.

BACKGROUND

Approximately one-fifth of the U.S. workforce now requires a license or certificate to work in their occupation, compared with 5 percent in the 1950s (Kleiner and Krueger 2013). Data from the 2019 U.S. Current Population Survey estimates that nearly 22 percent of all employed workers need a license, and nearly 23 percent of workers in the "Other services" category, which includes personal beauty services, require a license. Licensing is often associated with higher consumer prices, a fall in the labor supply, and higher profits for licensed providers (Dorsey 1983; Hogan 1983; Kleiner 2000; White House 2015).

Licensing also generates rents, which are earnings and revenue above the competitive market level, for workers in those occupations. Cosmetology licensing generates annual rents of about $1.7 billion (Adams, Jackson, and Ekelund 2002), while barber licensing increases barber earnings between 11 and 22 percent (Timmons and Thornton 2010). Licensing also can have a strong effect on immigrant communities. For example, higher licensing for manicurists reduced the number of Vietnamese manicurists by nearly 18 percent and led to community dispersion during the end of the twentieth century (Federman, Harrington, and Krynski 2006).

Legislatures and courts cite quality and consumer safety rationales when passing and upholding occupational licensing, as in *Meadows v. Odom* (2003) and *Vong v. Sansom* (2009) (Theiss 2011). Research on the impact of licensing on quality remains an important field of study. Licensing could potentially lower quality as suppliers face less competition, especially if consumers face asymmetric information or if reputational effects are weak (Leland 1979). The benefits of higher licensing also may generate higher prices for consumers and greater returns to the licensed workers as competition is restricted (Pagliero 2011). These restrictions may come at the cost of pricing other consumers out of the market (Carroll and Gaston 1983; Shapiro 1986). A major barrier to empirical research testing the link between licensing and quality has been the lack of available quality metrics across the more than 800 occupations licensed in at least one state (Kleiner and Krueger 2013).

There is some empirical evidence on the link between licensing and quality. Dentistry historically is a licensed profession, but more stringent licensing requirements were not found to improve dental outcomes, as evaluated with statutory data on licensing from 1960 to 1994 (Kleiner and Kudrle 2000). Recent evidence from online platforms shows that more stringent licensing does not improve quality for residential home services, as measured by consumer ratings, but that it does reduce competition and increase prices (Farronato et al. 2020). Licensing also may not affect quality in the same way across income groups. Child care licensing reduced the number of providers in low-income neighborhoods, estimated with data from 1987 to 2000, while increasing the quality of providers in high-income neighborhoods (Hotz and Xiao 2011), which represents a welfare transfer from low-income to high-income neighborhoods. Floral licensing, with florists rating floral arrangements, also did not significantly affect product quality in a 2010 test (Carpenter 2011, 2012). Similarly, I find that higher licensing requirements generally do not have a positive association with higher ratings. Higher licensing fees are negatively associated with ratings, with statistically significant results. The association between ratings and higher requirements for more education and experience is negative and statistically significant, but not economically large. Requiring more licensing exams is statistically significant for some subsamples; the association is negative for makeup artist licensing but positive for shampooer licensing. I also find that the breadth of licensing generally has significant negative effects on ratings, ranging from the economically small to changes in whole ratings for a business. I find that makeup artist licensing has a positive effect on quality for businesses with the largest number of reviews, but shampooer licensing has a negative trend for all businesses.

USING THE RATINGS AND LICENSING DATASETS

Using the Yelp Open Dataset

The challenge to estimating quality for beauty services first arises from the availability of data on service quality. Unlike in education (teachers) and health care (doctors), there are few ways to check the quality in beauty service industries. This study employs the publicly available business ratings data from the Yelp Open Dataset to estimate the effects of licensing on quality, using business ratings as a measure of quality via customer satisfaction.

Publicly available Yelp business ratings have been used in studies on reputation, business responsiveness, and even hospital care. They have also been used to improve hospital care as a supplement to traditional patient surveys (Bardach et al. 2013; Ranard et al. 2016), as well as to evaluate the impact of local economic policy (Glaeser, Kim, and Luca 2017) and gentrification (Glaeser, Kim, and Luca 2018). Business ratings can signal expected quality to consumers and signal information about the quality of their competitors to firms (Luca 2016). Yelp ratings have also been found to accurately measure quality as estimated by other sources (Luca 2016). The social networks of Yelp users have been used to estimate the effect of in-network recommendations, with social network friends being 67 percent more likely to visit the same restaurant within a year (Teng 2019).

There is also evidence that businesses change their behavior in response to public ratings, suggesting that firms believe consumers rely on ratings (Gergaud, Storchmann, and Verardi 2015; Luca 2016). Yelp prohibits businesses from paying for reviews or removing reviews. However, businesses offering customers incentives in exchange for good reviews could potentially influence their rating, so I test the sensitivity of the results by restricting businesses by their number of reviews. It is important to account for how many reviews a business has because the number of reviews in the sample varies considerably. For example, some businesses have as few as 3 reviews and some have over 600. The average rating for a business with only 10 reviews would be more influenced by the removal of a particular review, or the presence of a single one-star or five-star review, than the average rating for a business with

600 reviews. The number of reviews by quartile groups for the analysis samples is also discussed later in the chapter.

Organizing the Ratings Data

The ratings data were downloaded in February 2020 and exported from Python to a CSV file. Stata 16 was used for all data analysis. The original dataset includes 209,379 unique businesses with information on the business ID, name, location, average rating, number of reviews, whether or not the business is open, and the industries in which it operates. There is one observation and rating for each business. Average ratings are coded on a scale of one to five stars with half-star points. Ratings cannot be broken down over time, although the number of reviews captures information about how established the business is, for example, by age or reputation. The data include businesses with at least 3 reviews. Location data include the business' address, city, state, postal code, and latitude and longitude. The industry data include a list of industries for the business; for example, a barbershop may be cross-listed under both hair salons and men's hair salons.

To identify the businesses that face licensing requirements for makeup artists or shampooers, as well as businesses that offer pet grooming, I identified businesses using the industry string variable. Makeup artists may work independently or in salons, and the industry variable includes a separate identification for makeup artists. I did not include permanent makeup services, which is a separate service. Shampooers work in salons. To minimize potential errors from businesses that primarily provide hair styling, I restricted the sample for shampooer licensing to businesses listed under hair salons. Pet groomers may work in a variety of pet-service-related businesses, but the industry variable includes a separate identification for pet groomers.[1]

In addition, I rescaled the five-star average rating variable to a nine-point ordinal scale for regression analysis, i.e., one star is equal to one on the ordinal scale, but one-and-a-half stars is equal to two on the ordinal scale, two stars is equal to three on the ordinal scale, etc.

OCCUPATIONAL LICENSING DATA

There is often frequent overlap in the services provided in beauty salons, all of which may face licensing requirements. For example, a beauty salon may employ a cosmetologist, an esthetician, a makeup artist, a shampooer, a waxing specialist, and an eyebrow threader. Workers in each of these specialized occupations can face licensing requirements, although some statutes are now being struck down on a state-by-state basis (Sibilla 2020). In other cases, states are trying to expand requirements (Herbert 2018; Ziv 2020). Although barbers and cosmetologists are universally licensed in the United States, makeup artists are licensed in 41 states and shampooers are licensed in 37 states (Carpenter et al. 2017). According the 2017 U.S. Census, there are an estimated 78,887 beauty salon establishments in the United States, with $22.6 billion in revenue and 432,037 employees.

This study uses state occupational licensing requirements from the License to Work dataset (Carpenter et al. 2017). The dataset includes licensing requirements for five categories across all 50 states and D.C. for 102 commonly licensed occupations. The five categories in the dataset are licensing fees, requirements for education and experience in days, the number of state-required licensing exams (both practical and written), the minimum school grade, and the minimum age requirement. I focus on the first three categories in this study, as minimum school grade and age requirements most often correlate with high school graduation and the age of majority. I also use the log licensing fees for the analysis.

Makeup artists apply cosmetics to the face or other exposed body areas in order to alter an individual's appearance; they are licensed in 41 states. The occupation is ranked as having the fifty-eighth most burdensome licensing requirements and as being the twenty-eighth most widely and onerously licensed occupation (Carpenter et al. 2017). Louisiana and Nevada specifically license makeup artists—the other 39 states license makeup application under the scope of licenses administered by cosmetology boards (Carpenter et al. 2017). On average, makeup artist licensing requires $169 in fees, 134 days of education and experience, and successful completion of two licensing exams. Wisconsin requires the most licensing fees in this sample, at $391, and Illinois requires the most days of education and experience, with 175 days.

Shampooers shampoo and rinse customers' hair and are licensed in 37 states. The occupation is ranked as having the forty-fifth most burdensome requirements and as being the thirty-second most widely and onerously licensed occupation. Of the 37 states that license shampooers, Alabama, Louisiana, Nevada, New Hampshire, South Carolina, Tennessee, and West Virginia specifically license shampooers. The other 30 states license shampooing under the scope of licenses administered by barbering and cosmetology boards (Carpenter et al. 2017). On average, shampooer licensing requires $130 in licensing fees, 248 days of education and experience, and successful completion of two licensing exams. Wisconsin requires the most licensing fees in this sample at $391, and Ohio requires the most days of education and experience with 280 days.

MERGING THE DATASETS

I first restricted the ratings data to observations that included all variables used in this analysis. I then identified the county for each business using the latitude and longitude variables and the 2019 TIGER county shapefiles and merged in the estimated 2019 county population data, all from the U.S. Census Bureau. State identifiers from the Census Bureau were then used to merge the consumer ratings data with the Carpenter et al. (2017) licensing requirements data. Separate files were created for the makeup artist and shampooer samples. In the second part of the analysis, which includes a modified difference-in-difference regression approach, I included pet groomers as an unlicensed comparison occupation for both makeup artists and shampooers. The final panel dataset of all three occupations included 7,224 businesses in eight states (Arizona, Illinois, North Carolina, Nevada, Ohio, Pennsylvania, South Carolina, and Wisconsin).[2]

METHODOLOGY

Identifying Treatment and Comparison States

After the sample of ratings and licensing requirements were merged, I identified the states that require any licensing for makeup artists and the states that require any licensing for shampooers. Figure 7.1 shows

Figure 7.1 States by Sample and Licensing

Makeup artists

Shampooers

☐ Not in sample
▨ In sample, not licensed
■ In sample, licensed

NOTE: There are 1,430 observations in states which require licensing for makeup artists and 574 observations in states which do not. There are 2,117 observations in states which require shampooer licensing and 4,197 observations in states which do not.

the state licensing maps for makeup artists and shampooers. The eight states in the sample are located across the four U.S. Census Regions. There is one state in Census Division 2 – Middle Atlantic (Pennsylvania); three states in Census Division 3 – East North Central (Illinois, Ohio, and Wisconsin); two states in Census Division 5 – South Atlantic (North Carolina and South Carolina); and two states in Census Division 8 – Mountain (Arizona and Nevada). Although the original dataset does not include all 50 states, and states are further restricted to businesses in the study occupations, the final dataset still includes a dispersion of states across the country.

Identifying the Distribution of Ratings by the Number of Reviews

The ratings data also report the number of reviews for each business. As the number of reviews may capture unobserved information about a business, such as the size of the customer base and whether the business is new, I restrict samples of businesses by the number of their reviews. I first compared the results of using all businesses to the results of those with at least 10 reviews, and then at least 30 reviews.[3] I also split the businesses into quartile groups with both lower and upper bounds based on the number of reviews. This method organizes businesses into similar groups by the number of their reviews, relative to everyone else in the sample.

THE EFFECT OF THE DEPTH OF LICENSING AND RATINGS

I first use a linear regression to estimate the relationship between ratings and the depth of licensing requirements. I only consider makeup artists and shampooers in this analysis and analyze each occupation separately. I estimate the relationship between the outcome of the scaled rating and the independent variables of logged licensing fees, education and experience requirements in days, and the number of licensing exams.[4] Figure 7.2 reports the results for the relationship between licensing requirements and ratings. Smaller confidence interval bands around the coefficient estimate represent higher degrees of statistical significance.

Figure 7.2 Estimates for the Level of Licensing on Ratings

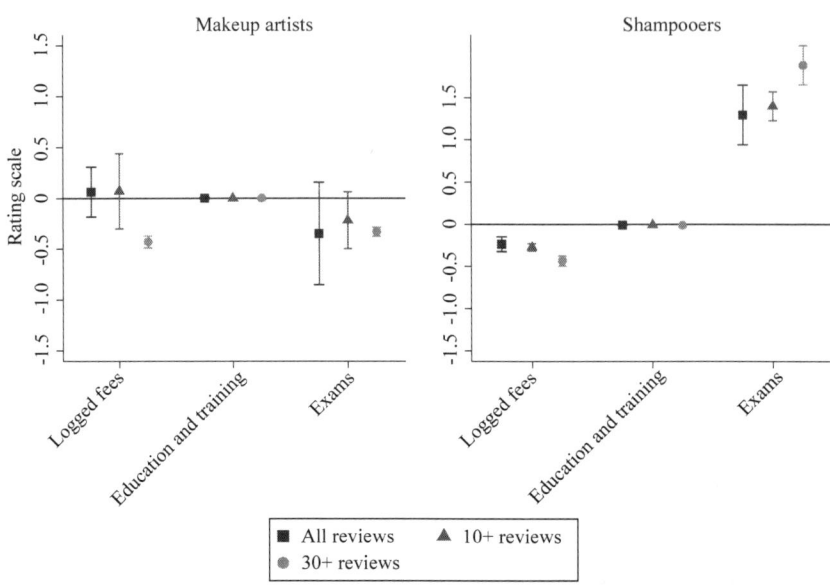

NOTE: Estimates were calculated using basic linear regression with standard errors clustered by county.
SOURCE: Data are publicly available business ratings from the Yelp Open Dataset and the 2017 License to Work dataset.

Requiring more licensing does not have a positive significant association with higher business ratings for makeup artists. When the sample is restricted to businesses with at least 30 reviews, there is a significant negative association for higher logged licensing fees of (-0.43 ± 0.02) and for more licensing exams (-0.33 ± 0.02). The estimates for education and experience were positive and significant but not economically different from zero. This suggests that licensing imposes costs on makeup artists and their customers without increasing quality. For example, increasing licensing fees by 5 percent would be associated with about a whole star reduction in a business rating, such as from three stars to two stars.[5]

The estimates for the association between ratings and shampooer licensing indicate a significant negative association between higher logged licensing fees for all three samples, with estimates between

−0.23 (±0.04) and −0.43 (±0.03). In contrast, there is a positive sig-nificant association for licensing exams for all three samples, with esti-mates from 1.3 (±0.17) and 1.89 (±0.10). The estimates for education and experience were negative and significant but not economically dif-ferent from zero. In this case, the costs from licensing are partially off-set by the quality gains from licensing exams, although there are still quality losses from higher licensing fees.

THE EFFECT OF ANY LICENSING ON RATINGS

Next I estimate the relationship between ratings and the presence of licensing requirements. I estimate the effects of licensing by comparing the ratings for makeup artists (both licensed and unlicensed) and sham-pooers (both licensed and unlicensed) with the ratings for pet groomers, who face no licensing requirements in the sample. I identify whether businesses are in states that require licensing for their occupation and estimate the effect of licensing on ratings using these characteristics.[6]

Figure 7.3 reports the effect of licensing on quality, presented by the minimum number of reviews for businesses. The effect of licensing on ratings for makeup artists is negative for the sample with all businesses and those with at least 10 reviews, at which point it becomes significant (−0.19 ± 0.04). In contrast, the effect of licensing on ratings for busi-nesses with at least 30 reviews is positive (0.12 ± 0.04). However, both of these effects are economically small, such that requiring any licens-ing affects the rating by less than a full point on the ordinal scale. The effect of licensing on ratings for shampooers is similarly small, nega-tive, and not significant across all three samples. At best, this suggests that licensing has no general positive effect on quality.

Figure 7.4 reports another test on the effect of licensing on quality, presented by quartile groups for the number of reviews for businesses.[7] I include results for the full sample as before, as well as the results of a restricted sample. The full sample for makeup artists includes the fol-lowing number of reviews by group: Group I (3–5 reviews); Group II (6–11); Group III (12–28); and Group IV (29–646). The full sample for shampooers includes the following number of reviews by group: Group I (3–5 reviews); Group II (6–9); Group III (10–23); and Group

Figure 7.3 The Effect of Licensing on Ratings, by Number of Reviews

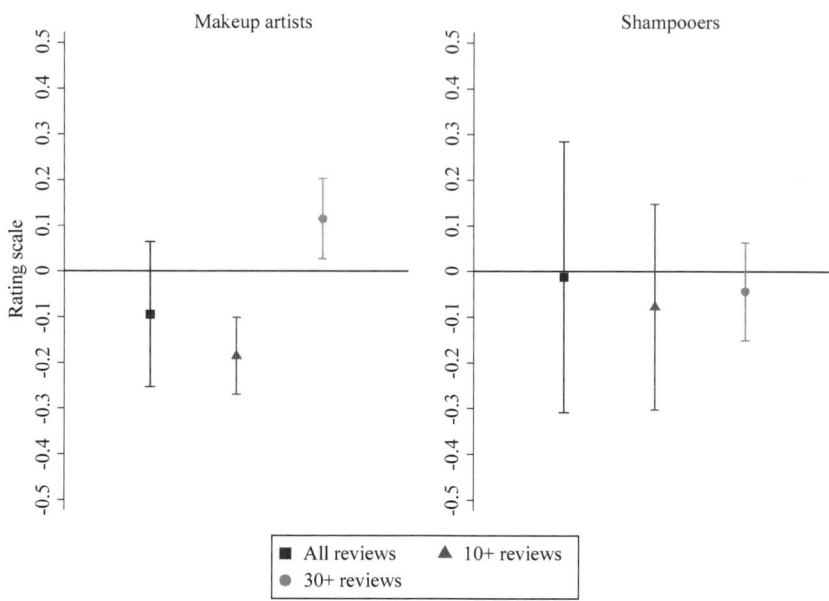

NOTE: Estimates were calculated on the scaled rating using a difference-in-differences linear regression with standard errors clustered by county.

SOURCE: Data are publicly available business ratings from the Yelp Open Dataset and the 2017 License to Work dataset.

IV (24–649). The restricted sample for makeup artists includes the following number of reviews by group: Group I (3–6 reviews); Group II (7–15); Group III (16–43); and Group IV (44–646). The restricted sample for shampooers includes the following number of reviews by group: Group I (3–5 reviews); Group II (6–10); Group III (11–26); and Group IV (27–649).

Of the 41 states that license makeup artists, Nevada grants a specific license for the occupation, and of the 37 states that license shampooers, Nevada and South Carolina similarly grant a specific license (Carpenter et al. 2017).[8] Because the cross-licensing from cosmetology may affect the results, I tested the findings by restricting the samples to states that either did not license the occupation and those that specifically grant a

Figure 7.4 The Effect of Licensing on Ratings, by Review Quartile Group

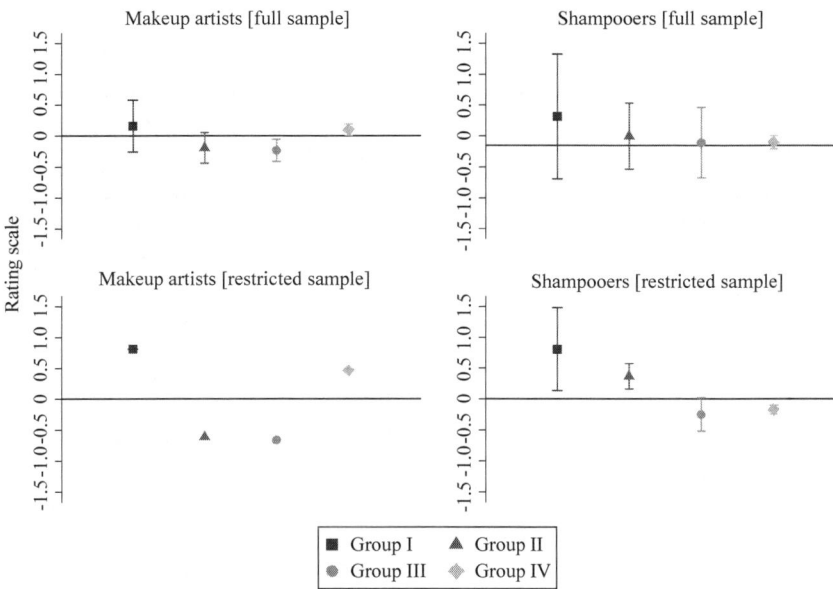

NOTE: Groups I to IV represent the quartile groups by the number of reviews for businesses. The restricted sample drops states which license makeup artists or shampooers under cosmetology from the treatment group. Estimates were calculated on the scaled rating using a difference-in-differences linear regression with standard errors clustered by county.

SOURCE: Data are publicly available business ratings from the Yelp Open Dataset and the 2017 License to Work dataset.

license to the occupation. Pet groomers are still used as the comparison occupation. The results are similar to the previous tests of the effect of licensing on quality, with significant positive effects for makeup artists with few (Group I) and many (Group IV) reviews and negative effects for those in the midrange (Groups II and III). The results for shampooers follow the same trend as in the full sample; however, the results are statistically significant for Groups I, II, and IV.

DISCUSSION

I find that licensing requirements, either by depth or breadth, do not significantly increase quality through the ratings measure of consumer satisfaction. I do find evidence that licensing sometimes has a negative effect on quality—this result is clearer when businesses are separated by the number of reviews. At best, licensing does not seem to measurably increase quality across the board or for all businesses, even within the same occupation. At worst, licensing barriers reduce quality while also imposing entry barriers for workers and higher costs for consumers.

The number of reviews for a business can significantly affect its average rating, especially when comparing businesses with very few reviews to those with many. Therefore, the number of reviews serves as a useful way to differentiate and group businesses by review size. This study finds that licensing increases quality for makeup artists with very few or very many reviews. The results for shampooer licensing also follow a negative trend across the distribution, which is even more interesting when considering that shampooers are often licensed with cosmetologists, who are universally licensed. Considered together, licensing may be reducing average quality for the average licensed business.

However, not all types of licensing requirements had the same effect. Licensing exams may verify that applicants actually meet a quality threshold, whereas licensing fees would instead impose a financial threshold. Education and experience surprisingly seem to have no economically significant effect on quality, because although the results are statistically significant, the magnitude effect on ratings is indistinguishable from zero. Despite makeup artists and shampooers having to complete hundreds of days of education and experience, it has not led to measurably higher quality. Pet groomers, after all, similarly stand on their feet much of the day and shampoo and style their client's appearance. If licensing requirements for human beauty services are not leading to higher-quality services than those of unlicensed pet beauty services, it is perhaps worth evaluating the costs of licensing against its promised benefits.

Ultimately, the major finding is that licensing does not seem to reliably increase quality, as measured by consumer ratings. This result may not be surprising, given that many businesses are grandfathered into new licensing requirements (Han and Kleiner 2021), which raises further questions about the efficacy of licensing in raising quality or protecting public health and safety. However, the results for beauty service occupations are new, and given the prevalence of beauty service licensing requirements, relevant to policy reform. Further research on this subject is warranted as more data on changes in licensing over time becomes available.

There are some limitations to this study. Businesses were matched as closely as possible with occupational licensing requirements, but given cross-licensing within beauty service occupations, the estimates in this study may underestimate the effects of licensing on quality. The study also cannot control for unobservable changes over time, either from changes in a business' rating over time or changes in licensing requirements. I also cannot tell if there are unlicensed businesses in my sample that are evading licensing requirements in their state. However, there are strong incentives for producers outside the legal market to avoid publicity. Also, there is no way to determine if businesses select on licensing requirements in a state based on the quality of service they intend to produce. Some of these challenges are common to licensing studies and studies that use the Yelp Open Dataset.

OPPORTUNITIES FOR LICENSING REFORM

In spring of 2020, as states began shutting down social and economic activity in an effort to curb the spread of COVID-19, they also began waiving requirements and expanding scope of practice for healthcare workers (Timmons, Bayne, and Norris 2020). Proponents of licensing argue that the regulation protects the public health and safety, and yet during a pandemic, states prioritized fast-tracking and waiving licensure requirements, expanding scope of practice, and recognizing out-of-state licenses for health care services. Regulatory reforms to other sectors also emerged, such as allowing customers to order alcohol with their food delivery, as states recognized businesses were struggling to stay open (Gonzalez 2018). At the same time, many beauty salons, including hair salons and nail salons, waited months longer to reopen (Sandler 2020).

Licensing reform for beauty services is not a minor undertaking or one without high stakes for practitioners. In 2020, New York State legislators advanced a bill that would mandate a new shampoo assistant certificate. Prospective shampooers would have to complete a minimum of 500 hours of the required 1,000 hours in a licensed school, pay a fee, and would be subject to a civil penalty of $500 for the first violation and $1,000 for subsequent violations (Ziv 2020). The bill also includes the fiscal impact and notes that the licensing requirement would generate revenue for the state in the form of licensing fees and civil penalties, which may raise questions about the motivation behind such requirements. State regulatory agencies are being presented with new opportunities to reform occupational licensing and increase access to labor markets, which many states did for health care workers early on in the COVID-19 pandemic.

Instead of increasing licensing requirements, states could recognize licenses that were granted by other states. States could also engage in licensing reciprocity agreements, which allows for mutual recognition of licenses from other states. These reforms could facilitate labor mobility and encourage new business at a time when such opportunities are desperately needed. State policy reform could also address the stringency of the occupational licensing requirements for beauty services, including makeup artists and shampooers. States could delicense the occupation or relax the requirements. Forty-one states license makeup artists and 37 states license shampooers, including those that license the occupations as part of cosmetology. The extent of beauty service licensing across states also represents the potential for large gains from policy reform in the way of increased access to labor markets without sacrificing consumer quality.

Conventional wisdom holds that occupational licensing protects public health and safety and thus raises quality. However, research has indicated small to neutral effects of licensing on quality, and in other cases, distributional effects between low- and high-income groups (Anderson et al. 2020). The analysis here suggests that licensing can, in contrast to expectations, lower quality, especially as measured by consumer satisfaction via ratings. State policy reform that reduces licensing barriers does not have to come at the cost of lower quality for consumers. Reforming licensing requirements could encourage greater labor mobility and economic opportunity for workers while also maintaining—or even improving—the quality of services for consumers.

Notes

1. I dropped Yelp pet groomer businesses cross-listed under "Veterinarians," as veterinarians are licensed separately. I also dropped observations that had potential mistakes in the list of the businesses' industries, such as "Entertainment" or "Jewelry." These cross-listings may occur because businesses are located in shopping centers or are otherwise cross-listed.
2. The original Yelp Open Dataset sample included 27 states. I restricted the sample to states that had at least 30 observations and included observations for both the licensed and unlicensed occupations.
3. Kernel density estimates for ratings were calculated using the Epanechnikov kernel function.
4. In the scaled rating, a rating of 5 stars is equal to 9 points, a rating of 4.5 stars is equal to 8 points, etc. I control for the county population and cluster standard errors by county. Estimates are reported at the 95 percent confidence level.
5. This model assumes a linear monotonic relationship between ratings and licensing. There may be diminishing marginal returns to level changes in licensing requirements that are not tested here.
6. I control for the county population and cluster standard errors by county. Estimates are reported at the 95 percent confidence level.
7. The model follows the same format as in the previous set of regressions.
8. Additional states grant specific licenses but are not in the sample.

References

Adams, A., III. Frank, John D. Jackson, and Robert B. Ekelund, Jr. 2002. "Occupational Licensing in a 'Competitive' Labor Market: The Case of Cosmetology." *Journal of Labor Research* 23(2): 261–278.

Anderson, D. Mark, Ryan Brown, Kerwin Kofi Charles, and Daniel I. Rees. 2020. "Occupational Licensing and Maternal Health: Evidence from Early Midwifery Laws." *Journal of Political Economy* 128(11): 4337–4383.

Bardach, Naomi S., Renée Asteria-Peñaloza, W. John Boscardin, and R. Adams Dudley. 2013. "The Relationship between Commercial Website Ratings and Traditional Hospital Performance Measures in the USA." *BMJ Quality & Safety* 22(3): 194–202.

Carpenter Dick M., II. 2011. "Blooming Nonsense: Do Claims about the Consumer Benefit of Licensure Withstand Empirical Scrutiny?" *Regulation* Spring: 44–47.

———. 2012. "Testing the Utility of Licensing: Evidence from a Field Experiment on Occupational Regulation." *Journal of Applied Business and Economics* 13(2): 28–41.

Carpenter, Dick M., II, Lisa Knepper, Kyle Sweetland, and Jennifer Mcdonald. 2017. *A National Study of Burdens from Occupational Licensing.* 2nd ed. Arlington County, VA: Institute for Justice.

Carroll, Sidney L., and Robert J. Gaston. 1983. "Occupational Licensing and the Quality of Service: An Overview." *Law and Human Behavior* 7(2–3): 139–146.

Dorsey, Stuart. 1983. "Occupational Licensing and Minorities." *Law and Human Behavior* 7(2–3): 171–181.

Farronato, Chiara, Andrey Fradkin, Bradley Larsen, and Erik Brynjolfsson. 2020. "Consumer Protection in an Online World: An Analysis of Occupational Licensing." NBER Working Paper No. 26601. Cambridge, MA: National Bureau of Economic Research.

Federman, Maya N., David E. Harrington, and Kathy J. Krynski. 2006. "The Impact of State Licensing Regulations on Low-Skilled Immigrants: The Case of Vietnamese Manicurists." *American Economic Review* 96(2): 237–241.

Gergaud, Olivier, Karl Storchmann, and Vincenzo Verardi. 2015. "Expert Opinion and Product Quality: Evidence from New York City Restaurants." *Economic Inquiry* 53(2): 812–835.

Glaeser, Edward, Hyunjin Kim, and Michael Luca. 2017. "Nowcasting the Local Economy: Using Yelp Data to Measure Economic Activity." Cambridge, MA: National Bureau of Economic Research.

———. 2018. "Measuring Gentrification: Using Yelp Data to Quantify Neighborhood Change." NBER Working Paper No. 24952. Cambridge, MA: National Bureau of Economic Research.

Gonzalez, Sarah. 2018. "Does Alcohol To Go Have a Chance to Survive the Pandemic?" *All Things Considered*, National Public Radio, September 18. https://www.npr.org/2020/09/18/914519464/does-alcohol-to-go-have-a-chance-to-survive-the-pandemic (accessed December 16, 2021).

Han, Suyoun, and Morris M. Kleiner. 2021. "Analyzing the Influence of Occupational Licensing Duration and Grandfathering on Wage Determination." *Industrial Relations* 60(2): 147–187.

Herbert, Danedri. 2018. "Occupational License for Eyebrow Threading?" *The Sentinel*, February 25. https://sentinelksmo.org/occupational-license-for-eyebrow-threading/ (accessed December 15, 2021).

Hogan, Daniel B. 1983. "The Effectiveness of Licensing: History, Evidence, and Recommendations." *Law and Human Behavior* 7(2–3): 117–138.

Hotz, V. Joseph, and Mo Xiao. 2011. "The Impact of Regulations on the Supply and Quality of Care in Child Care Markets." *American Economic Review* 101(5): 1775–1805.

Kleiner, Morris M. 2000. "Occupational Licensing." *Journal of Economic Perspectives* 14(4): 189–202.

Kleiner, Morris M., and Alan B. Krueger. 2013. "Analyzing the Extent and Influence of Occupational Licensing on the Labor Market." *Journal of Labor Economics* 31(2): S173-S202.

Kleiner, Morris M., and Robert T. Kudrle. 2000. "Does Regulation Affect Economic Outcomes? The Case of Dentistry." *Journal of Law and Economics* 43(2): 547–582.

Leland, Hayne E. 1979. "Quacks, Lemons, and Licensing: A Theory of Minimum Quality Standards." *Journal of Political Economy* 87(6): 1328–1346.

Luca, Michael. 2016. "Reviews, Reputation, and Revenue: The Case of Yelp. Com." Working Paper No. 12–016. Cambridge, MA: Harvard Business School.

Meadows v. Odom, 03-960-B-2 (2003).

Pagliero, Mario. 2011. "What Is the Objective of Professional Licensing? Evidence from the U.S. Market for Lawyers." *International Journal of Industrial Organization* 29(4): 473–483.

Ranard, Benjamin L., Rachel M. Werner, Tadas Antanavicius, H. Andrew Schwartz, Robert J. Smith, Zachary F. Meisel, David A. Asch, Lyle H. Ungar, and Raina M. Merchant. 2016. "Yelp Reviews of Hospital Care Can Supplement and Inform Traditional Surveys of the Patient Experience of Care." *Health Affairs* 35(4): 697–705.

Sandler, Rachel. 2020. "California Reopens Indoor Hair Salons, Malls—But Gyms, Churches Still Have to Stay Outdoors." *Forbes*, August 28.

Shapiro, Carl. 1986. "Investment, Moral Hazard, and Occupational Licensing." *Review of Economic Studies* 53(5): 843–862.

Sibilla, Nick. 2020. "New Law Lets Hair and Makeup Artists Work without a License in Minnesota." *Forbes*, May 28.

Teng, Hao. 2019. "Social Networks and Consumption Behavior: Evidence from Yelp." Unpublished working paper.

Theiss, Evelyn. 2011. "When It Comes to Pedicures, State Agency Keeps Nail Salons on Their Toes." *Cleveland.com*, August 22. https://www.cleveland.com/healthfit/2011/08/state_agency_keeps_nail_salons.html (accessed December 15, 2021).

Timmons, Edward J., Ethan Bayne, and Conor Norris. 2020. "A Primer on Emergency Occupational Licensing Reforms for Combating COVID-19." Mercatus Center Policy Brief. Arlington, VA: Mercatus Center, George Mason University.

Timmons, Edward, and Robert Thornton. 2010. "The Licensing of Barbers in the USA." *British Journal of Industrial Relations* 48(4): 740–757.

Vong v. Sansom, 037208 (2009).

White House. 2015. "Occupational Licensing: A Framework for Policymakers." Washington, DC: The White House.

Ziv, Shahar. 2020. "New York Proposes 500 Hour Training Hurdle to Become Shampoo Assistant, Despite Soaring Unemployment." *Forbes*, September 18.

8
Concluding Thoughts and Policy Recommendations

Maria Koumenta

Queen Mary, University of London and
Knee Center for the Study of Occupational Regulation

The key public policy justification for occupational licensing is its presumed ability to protect the general public from incompetent and unscrupulous practitioners. Consumers often lack the knowledge to assess the quality of a product or service prior to purchasing it, particularly if it is technical or requires specialist knowledge or skills. By setting minimum qualification requirements for entry to occupations, occupational licensing is expected to raise average skills and competence levels in the occupation, since low-quality providers will likely be unable to meet the new qualification requirements and therefore driven out of the occupation (Pagliero 2013; Rostam-Afschar 2014). Taken together, entry regulations are expected to ensure that consumers receive a more homogeneous and high-quality product, while the resulting higher investments in training have the potential to enhance the skills base in the labor market. If this is the case, then the well-documented negative labor market effects of occupational licensing need to be weighed against the potentially positive service quality and efficiency effects it yields in their markets and by extension to the wider economy.

There is little known about the empirical relationship between regulation of occupations and quality of services. This book makes an important contribution to knowledge of the quality and efficiency effects of regulation. We study six markets (ridesharing, driving instruction, pharmacies, beauty services, legal services, and health care) in four European countries (Poland, Italy, Ireland, and the United Kingdom) and the United States, as well as exploiting specific features in each regulated market using novel approaches.

GREASE OR GRIT?

How does occupational regulation affect quality? Here we present a summary of the results; see Table 8.1. We find no evidence that more stringent licensing for ridesharing drivers has an effect on customer satisfaction ratings or measures of hard braking and accelerations. An increase in regulations pushed many driving instructors out of the market and increased prices but did not improve the quality of instructors or success rates for learner drivers. In the pharmacy market, the availability of pharmacies seems to be correlated with a decrease in the number of hospital admissions related to influenza, suggesting a possible link to the accessibility of the services offered by pharmacists and consumer health. With legal services, there was little change in the overall quality of legal services following Polish relaxation of entry requirements as measured by complaints and disciplinary cases, and the availability of practitioners in the market increased. We find considerable variation in how rigidly defined and inflexible the scope of practice is among medical practitioners across different U.S. states, while a systematic review of the empirical literature shows that allowing medical practitioners the ability to work independently from physicians does not reduce the quality of care. Finally, in beauty services, licensing requirements either by depth or breadth do not significantly increase quality as measured by consumer satisfaction ratings.

Taken together, these case studies indicate that an increase in the availability of service providers or competition does not have negative effects on the quality of the services provided or survey measures of consumer satisfaction. To the contrary, in a number of cases we find positive effects of increased availability and competition. Our overarching conclusion is that licensing regulations in the occupational markets we studied serve more as grit than grease in driving efficiency and quality. This contrasts with the strong opposition that policymakers typically face from professional associations and licensing boards when trying to implement reforms. Such opposition perhaps is motivated more by the professionals' interests than by the interests of consumers, which are seldom arranged into influential and organized advocacy groups.

Table 8.1 Summary of Findings

Occupation and country	Nature of regulatory reform	Quality indicator	Summary of findings
Ridesharing drivers (London and Dublin)	Explore variations in the stringency of the regulatory regime between the two jurisdictions	Customer satisfaction ratings Hard braking and hard accelerations	No effects
Driving instructors (U.K.)	Increase in educational requirements to practice	Service availability indicators Indicators of student performance Price levels	No effect on the quality of instructors Negative effect on outcomes for learner drivers Higher prices
Pharmacists (Italy)	Relaxation of quantitative and structural restrictions	Availability of pharmacies at the municipality level Health indicators	Positive effect on pharmacy availability and health indicators
Advocates and legal advisors (Poland)	Relaxation of restrictions relating to educational requirements to practice	Complaints and disciplinary cases Employment creation	Decrease in complaints and disciplinary cases against practitioners Positive effect on availability of practitioners
Health service practitioners (U.S.)	Relaxation on restrictions on the scope to practice	Health outcomes (e.g., mental health, child mortality, patient mortality rates) Price levels	Positive effect on health outcomes No effect on prices
Makeup artists and shampooers (U.S.)	State variation in licensing requirements	Satisfaction ratings by consumers	No effect of licensing on service quality

DIRECTIONS FOR RESEARCH

Nevertheless, while the debate continues among those who support regulation and those who argue for less, there is little acknowledgment of several fundamental questions that are central to these discussions: What are the underlying rationales for regulating occupations? Are current regulatory arrangements still serving effectively? How are advances in knowledge and technology changing markets and the availability of information, and thus the relationship between consumers and producers? What implications do regulations have for the current legal framework? Still, our work does not provide the last word on these issues. Although we offer a series of examples on how to approach the issue of measuring quality and how to use existing data to investigate the impact of regulation on quality. As with any empirical work, it is difficult to extrapolate from a sample or case, and more work is certainly needed on the consumer benefits and costs of occupational licensing.

How do you measure quality? Our work clearly shows that not only is it difficult to calculate, but even the very definition of quality varies greatly across and within markets. The quality of some services can be verified before purchase, while for other services verification comes during or after provisions of the service. For some services, quality can be verified only if additional costs are incurred, or not at all. Complaints and disciplinary cases for legal professionals; product availability and health outcomes for pharmacists; service availability and pass rates for driving instructors; infant mortality, care quality, and emergency room visits for health professionals; customer satisfaction surveys for beauty professionals; and hard accelerations and braking for ridesharing drivers as proxies for safety—these are all examples of the different meanings that the idea of quality might take in different service markets. Moreover, in most markets, quality is multidimensional, and even a longer list of measures might not capture the full experience of a customer. Still, we take on the challenge and try to measure quality using the available information. While admittedly imperfect, the long list of measures used throughout the book provides a variety of sources of information on quality upon which others can build..

To estimate the impact of regulation on quality, one needs not only measures of quality, but also variability in the intensity of regulation.

Our case studies focus on a number of reforms, but also exploit variability across different jurisdictions. An important lesson from our work is that there is more than one way to approach this empirical question. A strength of the empirical work presented in this volume is the use of a rich variety of data sources which came in the form of individual data from service satisfaction surveys (lawyers/beauticians), administrative data (pharmacists/legal professionals/health professionals), labor force survey data (driving instructors), and even big data from a giant in the gig economy (ridesharing drivers).

Since the main obstacle to studying the relationship between regulation and quality is a lack of data, there could be significant benefits from more systematic data collection. Surveys, for example, can serve as a useful tool to collect records on consumer satisfaction in a variety of service markets. The survey approach has the advantage of providing comparable data across nations and over time but has the disadvantage of capturing subjective evaluations. More objective quality measures are generally occupation- and country-specific. These could be systematically collected with the collaboration of the professional associations or regulatory agencies in each jurisdiction. Regulatory agencies should always attempt to evaluate regulatory changes that could affect service quality, as well as prices and employment. Anticipating the need to evaluate policy changes, forward-looking regulatory agencies could then start collecting the appropriate data before the reform. More generally, they could implement it in such a way that evaluation ex post becomes easier. Finally, consumer associations could play an active role in monitoring the quality of services in many markets. They are in a unique and privileged position to collect information on quality of services, as they have a direct link with the final users.

DIRECTIONS FOR POLICY

A common theme that emerged from the six case studies is that increasing the stringency of regulation is not necessarily associated with better quality outcomes for consumers. Removing licensing requirements or moving to a lighter touch could be a suitable policy lever for certain occupational groups. However, policy reform does not necessarily have to come in the form of delicensing. For example, we know from historical and institutional analyses of licensing that barriers to entry tend to be imposed cumulatively over time on occupations. Such barriers can progressively mount up to represent significant hurdles to entry: unnecessarily lengthy training, limits on the number of professionals that are allowed to operate in the market, restrictions on corporate forms that businesses can take, restrictions on joint exercise of professions, and scope of practice among occupations. Reexamining the depth and the breadth of licensing arrangements on an occupation-by-occupation basis could be a fruitful way to detect either redundant or excessive constraints that have become institutionalized. Indeed, as some of the authors in this volume point out, the COVID-19 pandemic made salient some of the inefficiencies of licensing regimes and how these in turn compromise quality and availability. Policymakers could seize this opportunity to reevaluate the extent to which this labor market institution influences the economy, and how it has evolved to serve its intended purposes for consumers.

Proponents of regulation argue that in markets where consumers cannot observe the quality of professionals, the imposition of a minimum quality standard through licensing will address the market failure resulting from asymmetric information. The underlying assumption is that asymmetric information is relevant and that professional regulation serves the public interest. This certainly is a powerful argument, albeit one that—as we have shown in this book—must be balanced against the fact that these regulations may raise prices for consumers and compromise service availability. A fruitful line of enquiry that regulators can pursue is whether there are alternative ways that the problem of asymmetric information can be addressed. Information technology, for example, has improved consumers' access to information about the quality of practitioners themselves (e.g., online reviews in digital platforms). Similarly, in some markets the availability of technical information can make consumers more knowledgeable about the services they receive, thus enabling them to better assess its quality. Overall, the availability of quality checks reduces the level of regulatory stringency needed to ensure the same service quality as in a world where the option to access this information was unavailable. Harnessing such alternatives is a fruitful path for policymakers to take.

References

Pagliero, Mario. 2013. "The Impact of Potential Labor Supply on Licensing Exam Difficulty." *Labour Economics* 25(C): 141–152.

Rostam-Afschar, Davud. 2014. "Entry Regulation and Entrepreneurship: A Natural Experiment in German Craftsmanship." *Empirical Economics* 47(3): 1067–1101.

Authors

Kihwan Bae is a research associate at the Knee Center for the Study of Occupational Regulation, West Virginia University.

Piotr Białowolski is an associate professor at Kozminski University and a research associate at the Sustainability and Health Initiative for NetPositive Enterprise (SHINE) at the Harvard TH Chan School of Public Health.

Darwyyn Deyo is an assistant professor of economics at San José State University, and an affiliate scholar at the Knee Center for the Study of Occupational Regulation at West Virginia University.

Morris M. Kleiner is a professor at the Humphrey School of Public Affairs, and he teaches at the Center for Human Resources and Labor Studies, both at the University of Minnesota–Twin Cities.

Maria Koumenta is an assistant professor of labor economics at Queen Mary, University of London, and a senior research fellow at the Knee Center for the Analysis of Occupational Regulation.

Michał Masior is a member of the Legislative Process Research Centre at the Faculty of Law and Administration, Lazarski University.

Eva Pagano is an adjunct professor at the University of Turin.

Mario Pagliero is a professor of economics at the University of Turin and a research fellow at the Collegio Carlo Alberto.

Emanuele Pivetta is an assistant professor in internal medicine at University of Turin, Department of Medical Sciences, and a staff physician at the Division of Emergency Medicine and High Dependency Unit of Città della Salute e della Scienza di Torino-Molinette hospital.

Lorenzo Richiardi is a professor of medical statistics at the University of Turin and director of the Cancer Epidemiology Unit of the University Hospital Città della Salute e della Scienza di Torino.

Edward Timmons is a service associate professor and director of the Knee Center for the Study of Occupational Regulation at West Virginia University.

Mark Williams is a professor in human resource management at Queen Mary, University of London.

Index

Note: The italic letters *f, n,* or *t* following a page number indicate a figure, note, or table, respectively, on that page. Double letters mean more than one such consecutive item on a single page.

About the Institute

The W.E. Upjohn Institute for Employment Research is a nonprofit research organization devoted to finding and promoting solutions to employment-related problems at the national, state, and local levels. It is an activity of the W.E. Upjohn Unemployment Trustee Corporation, which was established in 1932 to administer a fund set aside by Dr. W.E. Upjohn, founder of The Upjohn Company, to seek ways to counteract the loss of employment income during economic downturns.

The Institute is funded largely by income from the W.E. Upjohn Unemployment Trust, supplemented by outside grants, contracts, and sales of publications. Activities of the Institute comprise the following elements: 1) a research program conducted by a resident staff of professional social scientists; 2) the Early Career Research Award program, which provides funding for emerging scholars to complete policy-relevant research on labor-market issues; 3) a publications program and online research repository, which provide vehicles for disseminating the research of staff and outside scholars; 4) a regional team that conducts analyses for local economic and workforce development; and 5) the Employment Management Services Division, which administers publicly funded employment and training services as Michigan Works! Southwest in the Institute's local four-county area.

The broad objectives of the Institute's activities are to 1) promote scholarship and evidence-based practices on issues of employment and unemployment policy, and 2) make knowledge and scholarship relevant and useful to policymakers in their pursuit of solutions related to employment and unemployment.

Current areas of concentration for these programs include the causes, consequences, and measures to alleviate unemployment; social insurance and income maintenance programs; compensation and benefits; workforce skills; nonstandard work arrangements; and place-based policy initiatives for strengthening regional economic development and local labor markets.